The Israel Code

The Israel Code

Exploring the Past, Present and Future of Israel

David Clark

Austin Douglas Publications

THE ISRAEL CODE

© 2006 Austin Douglas Publications
Revised Edition
First Published in 2000 under the title:
Israel: Past, Present and Future

ISBN: 0-9550450-1-0

Printed in the United Kingdom by Creative Print and Design (Wales), Ebbw Vale.

1 2 3 4 5 6 7 8 9 10 / 09 08 07 06

Austin Douglas Publications
Greenacres
Downside Road
Backwell
Bristol
BS48 3EW

CONTENTS

This book is dedicated to the memory of my parents, Douglas and Dorothy Clark, without whose prayer and support I would not have come to know the one who is the past, present and future King of Israel, the Lord Jesus Christ.

PREFACE

This second edition of The Israel Code (formerly published as Israel, Past, Present and Future) has undergone radical revision. I am very appreciative of those who, by buying the first edition, forced me back to the drawing board as it were. The tenor of what I have written remains the same, but where the first edition made assumptions and might have been read almost as notes for discussion, I hope that this second edition makes the links between scriptures more obvious and also more readable.

Where I have thought it necessary, I have added chapters, particularly in the New Testament, where the role of a Jewish Messiah is central. I have also added maps in the last section which (I trust) help our understanding of the various kingdoms that have existed in the region.

I am indebted to the many people who have supported me in producing this second edition: to my wife Philippa for her ceaseless encouragement; Dr John Gillmore for his helpful textual suggestions; Ronna Fu for her cover design and David Jutsum, for so much work in preparation of the first and second drafts. Finally, my thanks are due to Noël Halsey and Linda Finley-Day of Summit Publishing for their patience, detailed input and wisdom which have transformed the book into its finished state.

INTRODUCTION

WHY WON'T ISRAEL GO AWAY?

". . . I have made you, you are My servant; O Israel, I will not forget you."

Isaiah 44:21

"' . . . I will restore you to health and heal your wounds,' declares the Lord, 'because you are called an outcast, Zion for whom no-one cares.'"

Jeremiah 30:17

Have you ever seen one of those investigative programmes on television? The ones where they finally track down the villain and he says; "Don't point that camera in my face, just go away. You're trespassing. This is my money, my property. Clear off!!"

Some sections of the Church have been like that when it comes to the promises God has made to Israel throughout His Word. All too often the assertion has been made: "This is ours now, we've inherited it, we've earned it. It's nothing to do with the nation of Israel. Go away!!"

To maintain their claims to the property (as it were), many individuals and churches have had to make false claims. They've scrawled across the original document, crossing out sections and forging a signature to prove it is theirs by right.

Quite often it's been done in ignorance. Someone told someone who told someone else and they said God had finished with the Jewish nation. They have never been back and looked at the original manuscript.

For many centuries it was possible for such people to argue that as Israel didn't exist anymore, God's Word concerning them applied only to Old Testament times. The re-emergence of the Jewish state of Israel in 1948, born out of the ashes of the holocaust, caused a seismic challenge to such attitudes; though many theologians have continued to dismiss modern-day Israel as an 'accident of history.'

It shouldn't surprise us. Since its inception thousands of years ago, Israel has been a challenge to man's rationale of what God should do. When we read the book of Revelation, we discover Israel will still be a stumbling block even after The Lord Jesus, the Messiah, returns to reign on earth.

In order to help us understand God's purposes, we need to go back to our source material, the Bible, and try and discover what God's Word really says. For us to do this, and so that we may understand something of where we stand in the history of God's purposes for Israel, I want to present a threefold view of Israel:

- Israel in Old Testament Times
- Israel in New Testament Times
- A brief history of the people and its land since the time of Jesus

It is not my intention to set out to talk about Israel or the Church, as though one is in opposition to the other; but rather to speak to us through these pages about Israel and the Church, each with a role in God's plan for the nations. At the same time, I hope that we can learn lessons that apply to us as individuals, churches and nations.

I should state from the outset that I believe this to be a

spiritual matter and not merely an academic exercise. If someone can persuade you something is right, you can be certain there is someone who can persuade you it is wrong. I start from the premise the Bible is the inspired Word of God, but I recognise that unless the Holy Spirit brings it alive to you, God's Word will remain as a series of stories—moral and upright without a doubt, but not life-changing.

It is up to you to make up your mind and to search scripture for yourself, to see whether what I have to say is right. I believe the message contained in this book is central to God's plans over the coming years. That alone makes it vital for our nations and our churches.

I also believe we should be challenged individually. The men and women we meet in its pages still speak to us about how God wants us to lead our lives. Micah, writing to a people in turmoil, said this: *"He has showed you, O man, what is good. And what does the LORD require of you? To act justly and to love mercy and to walk humbly with your God."*[1] May we respond to that cry as we read of God's plans and purposes for Israel in the coming days.

1   Micah 6:8

But now, this is what the LORD says—He who created you, O Jacob, He who formed you, O Israel:

"Fear not, for I have redeemed you; I have called you by name; you are Mine.

When you pass through the waters, I will be with you; and when you pass through the rivers, they will not sweep over you. When you walk through the fire, you will not be burned; the flames will not set you ablaze.

For I am the LORD, your God, the Holy One of Israel, your Saviour; I give Egypt for your ransom, Cush and Seba in your stead.

Since you are precious and honoured in My sight, and because I love you, I will give men in exchange for you, and people in exchange for your life.

Do not be afraid, for I am with you; I will bring your children from the east and gather them from the west.

I will say to the north, 'Give them up!' and to south, 'Do not hold them back.' Bring My sons from afar and My daughters from the ends of the earth—everyone who is called by My name, whom I created for my glory, whom I formed and made."

Lead out those who have eyes but are blind, who have ears but are deaf.

All the nations gather together and the peoples assemble. Which of them foretold this and proclaimed to us the former things? Let them bring in their witnesses to prove they were right, so that others may hear and say, "It is true."

"You are My witnesses," declares the LORD, "and My servant whom I have chosen, so that you may know and believe Me and understand that I am He. Before Me no god was formed, nor will there be one after Me.

I, even I, am the LORD, and apart from Me there is no saviour. I have revealed and saved and proclaimed—I, and not some foreign god among you. You are My witnesses," declares the LORD, "that I am God. Yes, and from ancient days I am He. No one can deliver out of My hand. When I act, who can reverse it?"

Isaiah 43: 1-13.

Chapter 1

THE CALL OF ABRAHAM

The LORD God formed the man from the dust of the ground and breathed into his nostrils the breath of life, and the man became a living being.

Genesis 2:7

The story of Israel begins, not with the calling of Abram, but many hundreds of years before, with the creation of Adam from the dust of the earth. God's amazing intention, even as creator, was that He would walk with man and make Himself known to man. In other words, that God and mankind would be able to exist in close friendship. For that to be fulfilled, and for us to be more than mere robots, God had to allow man to decide for himself whether what He said was true. He had to let man reason things out and make his own choices.

The most basic and simple questions were these:

- Was God telling the truth?
- Was God's Word reliable?

Those questions, and our response to them, are still at the heart of Christianity and they are at the heart of the history of Israel.

These central challenges lay at the core of Adam and Eve's choice in the Garden of Eden. For a while Adam and his wife lived in what can only be described as a paradise of close communion with God, until the day Eve encountered the serpent.

The Bible tells us: *the serpent was more crafty than any of the wild animals the Lord God had made.*[1] The serpent challenged God's Word to Adam and Eve by asking a leading question which he knew Eve would tell him wasn't true, in order to sow a seed of doubt in her mind. *"Did God really say,"* the serpent enquired (in a voice that must have oozed with apparent concern and interest), *'You must not eat from any tree in the garden?'*[2]

At this stage Eve should have dismissed him, but the serpent's approach was subtle; before Eve knew it she was engaged in conversation. She pointed out to Satan that what he'd said wasn't quite accurate. They were allowed to eat from all the trees in the garden except for one, which was placed at its centre. Should they eat from this one forbidden tree, then they would die. This was the opening the serpent was looking for and this was his reply: *"You will not surely die,"* the serpent said to the woman. *"For God knows that when you eat of it your eyes will be opened, and you will be like God, knowing good and evil."*[3]

This sowed enough seeds of doubt in Eve for her to have a close look at this forbidden fruit. She decided to examine the tree for herself, and saw that the fruit was attractive for three reasons:

- It was good for food
- It was pleasing to the eye
- It was desirable for gaining wisdom[4]

Those three reasons were enough to convince Eve. She ate the fruit and of course, once she had, she also persuaded Adam to eat. Satan was at least half-right (as he so often is) for their innocence was taken away. Their new-found knowledge made them aware that they were naked and conscious of the fact they had disobeyed the one commandment God had given them. The result was that Adam and Eve hid from God. Of course, it didn't do them any good, anymore than our

---

1   Genesis 3:1
2   Genesis 3:1
3   Genesis 3:4-5
4   Genesis 3:6

trying to hide from God can fool anyone except ourselves. The inevitable outcome of their disobedience was that God had to drive them from the Garden of Eden and from His presence, otherwise His just and holy judgement on their sin would have meant they both had to die. Adam and Eve were no longer able to talk with God in the way that they once had, but God was not prepared to write off the human race (His ultimate act of creation) because they had failed in the one area God had asked, obedience. He was still determined to reach out to them and to their descendants and so God took the skins of animals and covered Adam and Eve's nakedness; a symbol of the costly sacrifice that would ultimately be necessary for all mankind.

In the very real battle between good and evil that existed in the heavenlies, God knew there was only one thing that would wipe out man's sin and the weakness, sickness and death, now coursing through the human race. God had killed animals to provide clothing for Adam and Eve, but it would take a unique sacrifice for their sin to be totally blotted out. That sacrifice could only be worked out through the unjustified death of a man who lived a life of total obedience and righteousness. It would require a sacrifice from the Godhead to achieve it.

In total harmony of agreement, God the Father, God the Son and God the Holy Spirit determined to do just that and began to prepare the world for the coming of Jesus Christ, God's only Son. But in order to set the stage for these events to unfold, God knew he needed to find men whose hearts really yearned for Him. From them would come a nation who would be a visible demonstration, to the whole world, that God existed. That nation was the nation we know today as Israel.

Now we probably think that this could all have taken place in a matter of weeks, but God's idea of time and our own idea of time are somewhat different, probably because we're very conscious of how short our time on earth appears. In comparison, God sees our lives on this present earth as preparation for timeless existence, for everlasting life. We need to measure God's dealing with individuals and nations against this background, not against a 21st century world view that demands instant solutions.

It's very easy, when we read the Bible, to think of time in terms of chapters, but of course that is misleading. The lives of many figures in the Old Testament are summed up in a few verses, or even the mere mention of a name. When we read the history of Abraham's forefathers, we find that there are twenty generations from Adam to Abraham, covering a far greater period of time than we would see nowadays. From Adam, through Seth, Enoch, Noah, Eber and down to Abraham's father Terah, we cover some 1950 years of history. Here too, we find intriguing hints about the lives and hearts of men as they began to populate the earth.

God was looking for men who wanted to know Him—as he still does today. At the end of Genesis four, after we have been told of the birth of Seth's son Enoch, we read: *At that time men began to call upon* (or proclaim) *the name of the LORD.*[5] In the following chapter we read how Enoch, then aged 365, was taken to be with God. In Genesis six and seven we read the story of Noah, a man who—*found favour in the eyes of the LORD*[6]—and of whom God said; *"I have found you righteous in this generation."*[7]

These men however, were in the minority. While Noah and his family wanted to know God, the rebellion that had begun with Adam and Eve and continued through their descendants, reached such a pitch that the *earth was full of violence.*[8] God decided it was necessary to remove the rest of Noah's generation from the earth. God wasn't responding in a fit of pique but because *His heart was filled with pain,*[9] that those who had been created in His image should be acting in such

5   Genesis 4:26
6   Genesis 6:8
7   Genesis 7:1
8   Genesis 6:11
9   Genesis 6:6

a fashion. He had been patient with them for hundreds of years, but to no avail. In the midst of this generation, Noah stood out like a beacon.

I'm sure they mocked and laughed at Noah as he spent those lonely years building the ark to the exact plan God had laid out for him. Most men would have given up—but not Noah. He kept on in obedience, even though all around him life went on as it always had, and men jeered at the very idea of the existence of a God who would intervene in the running of the universe.

Noah's challenge is our challenge: we need to be obedient to God however foolish that may appear to be to those around us. We need to realise that ultimately, however patient God is with us and with our generation, God views sin seriously. Jesus himself warned that the world, on His return, would be in much the state it was at the time of the flood. *"Just as it was in the days of Noah, so also will it be in the days of the Son of Man. People were eating, drinking, marrying and being given in marriage, up to the day Noah entered the ark. Then the flood came, and destroyed them all."*[10]

Although the generations that followed the flood were direct descendants of Noah and must have heard graphic accounts about the catastrophe that had befallen the world, it didn't seem to make much difference. After Noah's death, as the world began to be re-populated, men met together to plan and build for a future that would be inspired by their own knowledge and understanding. As far as they were concerned, God had become an irrelevance.

The leading figures of the day decided to build an enormous tower which would be the symbol and centrepiece of all their efforts. That centrepiece was the tower of Babel. Once again God acted. So it was that the tower, intended as man's ultimate achievement, was instead thrown down, the single language of the world became confused and men were scattered over the

10   Luke 17:26-27

earth. Mankind's ambition to create his own system of knowledge and progress was thwarted; but it is also out of this unlikely and discouraging situation that, years later, Abram's father, Terah, comes to Haran and settles there.

> The challenge to Abram is the challenge to all Christians: Are we willing to put God's call on our lives before our family, personal comfort and security?

God had not forgotten his plan and purpose for mankind. The Bible refers to the heart of fallen man as, *'deceitful and beyond cure.'*[11] God's compassion however, reached beyond natural judgement and saw, in Terah's son Abram, what He had already seen in Enoch and Noah. Abram was a man of principle and obedience who wanted to re-establish the relationship with God that Adam had once enjoyed.

As we look through the dealings of God with the patriarchs (Abraham, Isaac and Jacob), it is important that we remember the design of God in all this. God's ultimate purpose, arising from a deep compassion that went beyond that natural judgement we have already mentioned, was to bring mankind back into relationship with Himself. He wanted to show the world that He was still at work on the earth. Even more importantly, He wanted to provide a certain means of escape, of salvation, for all mankind, through the perfect sacrifice of His Son, Jesus Christ.

That doesn't mean that everything else that happened or that God promised was irrelevant—far from it. But it does require an understanding of the central role of Jesus in all God's dealings with and through the land and nation of Israel.

---

11   Jeremiah 17:9

As we begin to examine God's dealings with Abram, we could perhaps entitle it; 'Receiving Some Promises and Leaving a Cultural Centre.' A much-loved friend of mine, Bill Bedford, who has now gone to be with the Lord, used to refer to Haran (where Abram was living), as being like an old university town. It's an apt description. It was, in fact, an important and flourishing city. It was a centre of culture and trade on the Balikh River, on the highway along which traders and, on occasion, armies marched.

Terah, Abram's father, had set out with the intention of going to Canaan, but having travelled six hundred miles he, his family and his grandson Lot arrived at Haran and settled there, still four hundred miles from their original destination.

The Bible is written very much in précis, giving us only the details essential for our understanding and knowledge of God's purposes. However, it's difficult to resist speculating why Terah began the journey in the first place. We know that he set out to go to Canaan, but we can only guess at what side-tracked him when he reached Haran. I suspect the setting of the city and its atmosphere of learning seduced Terah from his original purpose. Be that as it may, all we know with certainty is that Terah died there.[12]

Abram however, is commanded by God to leave Haran. The Lord said to Abram, *"Leave your country, your people and your father's household and go to the land I will show you."*[13] This required remarkable obedience on Abram's part. Not only did it mean leaving behind the comfort and prosperity of the city, but at this stage God had not even revealed where He was going to send him. God's command to go is the first test of Abram's faith.

It's very easy for us, when we are looking for guidance from God, to decide what we would like to do and rationalise our response in the light of circumstances. By contrast the challenge of faith is to:

12   Genesis 11:32
13   Genesis 12:1

- Be able to hear God's voice
- Act without knowing the full picture
- Be prepared to give up the comfortable for the uncomfortable
- Recognise that faith requires action

The challenge to Abram is the challenge to all Christians: Are we willing to put God's call on our lives before our family, our personal comfort and security?

God links the challenge with a promise: *"I will make you into a great nation and I will bless you; I will make your name great, and you will be a blessing. I will bless those who bless you, and whoever curses you I will curse; and all peoples on earth will be blessed through you."*[14]

God commits Himself to seven promises (five of which are in the first person) that He guarantees in response to Abram's obedience:

- Abram will become a great nation
- God will bless him
- Abram's name will be great
- Abram will be a blessing
- Blessings will follow those who bless him
- Curses will follow those who curse him
- Everyone on earth will be blessed through Abram

These are quite extraordinary statements and they ought to make us sit up and take very careful note when we read them. Here is Almighty God, committing Himself to a series of promises that are going to have repercussions for the whole earth.

The old United Kingdom passport used to 'require and request' safe passage for all British citizens. In the days of the Empire that normally carried some weight. What God says to Abram goes far, far beyond that. God tells Abram that even

---

14   Genesis 12:2-3

those who speak against him will find themselves judged. Lawyers would refer to this as an emphatic statement! As Christians we need to understand that God's Word is unchanging. Malachi tells us: *"I the LORD change not."*[15] When Balak, desperate to deal with the Israelites after they have left Egypt, offers Balaam a king's ransom to curse the gathered tribes, he is told; *"God is not a man, that He should lie, nor a son of man, that He should change His mind."*[16] Much as he might have liked to pocket Balak's reward, Balaam knows nothing he can say will change what God has decided to do.

The promises of those early verses of Genesis, made by God to Abram, are the first of a whole series of promises that we are going to find laid out for this remarkable individual. They come about because Abram lines his actions up with his faith and trusts God. Called by God, Abram sets out. There is a wonderful simplicity in the description given to this event. Abram, Sarai his wife and Lot (his nephew) together with their servants, possessions and flocks, are to travel the 400 miles to Canaan. The Bible sums the journey up with a single sentence: *They set out for the land of Canaan, and they arrived there.*[17] Unlike Terah, his father, Abram completes the journey on which he has embarked.

There is an important lesson in the simple statement recording that 400 mile journey, a far more hazardous undertaking than it would be for anyone contemplating it nowadays. What God call us to do, we need to complete. God will always keep His side of the agreement; we need to make sure we keep ours. Abram, in simple faith, had arrived where God intended him to be.

Having reached Canaan, Abram travels through the land, until he comes to what was at the time a famous landmark, the great tree of Moreh at Shechem. Although the land is occupied by the Canaanites God tells Abram; *"to your*

15   Malachi 3:6
16   Numbers 23:19
17   Genesis 12:5

offspring I will give this land."[18] While this again sounds very positive, if we analyse the statement we see this is a real test for Abram, the first major challenge since setting out. God is unpicking Abram's motives to make sure that what he is going to do will help fulfil God's pre-determined plans, not Abram's own ambitions. Having already been told that all the earth will be blessed through him, Abram might well have presumed that he would be involved in this enterprise and therefore he would see it through to conclusion. Now he discovers he is not to be the inheritor, but the catalyst for that inheritance in the distant future. It would have been very tempting for Abram to say, "But where's my reward?" rather than continue on in this adventure of faith.

We also need to realise that building what God has for our lives does not always mean we see the final outcome of our labour. Many people judge the success of Christian ministry by what they can see or measure physically. Abram was able to look beyond the immediate and see what God had for future generations. He wanted to do what God had called him to undertake. He would trust God to keep His promises and he would submit to God's plans and timing. As a result Abram was content to know God and to obey Him.

Time passed, and there was a famine in Canaan, so Abram went down to Egypt with his family. And here our man of God fails for the first time. He is afraid Sarai and he will get into trouble among these people, for his wife is considered very beautiful, so Abram pretends she is his sister. Technically he is right, for Sarai was in fact his half-sister, daughter of his father but not of his mother. Of course, Pharaoh is delighted, takes her into his palace and makes plans for her to be his wife. God however, protects Sarai and causes sickness to come upon Pharaoh's household. Discovering Abram's deceit, Pharaoh is horrified and sends Abram and Sarai away from the land.

18   Genesis 12:7

God intervenes, both on this occasion, and later when Abram repeats the lie to Abimelech, King of Gerar. God judges the men who want Sarai, and not Abram. To some this may seem unfair, but it is a wonderful picture of God's protection, even when our character lets us down. God continued to look at Abram's heart and knew he was committed to obedience, so Abram's weakness in allowing his wife to be put in danger was over-ridden by God's supernatural provision in the circumstances.

Why mention that when we are building up a picture of God's dealings with Abram and, ultimately, Israel? It's important because it shows us that God takes us as we are, with all our weaknesses and failings. When we come to God, in all our human imperfection, He is able to mature us into what He requires. It also shows us that even men of great faith have their limitations, can be afraid and can fail to look to God for protection.

Sometimes we imagine that God will only call the super-warriors or the outstandingly strong. That is not the case. It has never been the case with individuals, as we will see, and we need to remember it is not the case with Israel. It is a measure of God's compassionate nature that He reaches out to Israel in all her frailty.

Once the famine had ended, Abram returned to Canaan with his nephew Lot. This brings us to another defining moment in Abram's life: his dealings with his nephew. Lot's father had been a brother of Abram's. He had died in Ur of the Chaldeans,[19] the land of his birth. Reading between the lines we can presume that both Abram's father (Terah) and Abram, felt a special responsibility for looking after Lot, which is why Abram had taken him with his own family when they originally set out for Canaan.

Abram had become very wealthy[20] and both he and Lot had large flocks and herds. Over the course of time this led to

19   Genesis 11:28
20   Genesis 13:2

quarrels among their respective herdsmen. Abram, keen to avoid family arguments, suggested they part company.[21] As the older man, as the head of the household and as the one who was responsible for all the people with them, Abram could easily have pulled rank and told Lot just where he could (and could not) pasture his flocks and herds. He didn't—instead he offered Lot the choice. Lot, coming from a farming background, wasn't slow to see the advantages of the plain of Jordan, described as *like the garden of the LORD*, [22] and it didn't take him long to decide this was the area where he would like to live and take his flocks. Abram's generous and freely meant gesture, giving his nephew the best of the land, was not unnoticed by God. In response to it, God once again visited Abram and made him a new promise.

After Lot had separated from Abram and gone down to the Jordan Valley, God came and spoke to Abram: *"Lift up your eyes from where you are and look north and south, east and west. All the land that you see I will give to you and your offspring forever. I will make your offspring like the dust of the earth, that if anyone could count the dust, then your offspring could be counted. Go, walk through the length and the breadth of the land, for I am giving it to you."*[23]

Here we find God entering into a new covenant with Abram. This is not conditional upon Abram's future conduct, but is an absolute promise established through the mouth of God. Note the three promises about the land:

- It stretches in every direction as far as the eye can see
- All of the land is included
- It is an inheritance forever

When we buy a property, solicitors check to see if there are any other claims on the land, or whether it is freehold. Once we have bought it, we receive the title deeds and the house and the land attached to it become ours for our lifetime, or until we sell it or pass it on to someone else. But God says to

21   Genesis 13:8-9
22   Genesis 13:10
23   Genesis 13:14-17

Abram: this is not a conditional or lifetime guarantee, this is an inheritance forever. As far as God is concerned therefore, the ownership of the land is settled for all time. Anyone who wishes to dispute that has a quarrel with God, not with Abram's descendants.

A further promise accompanies this resounding declaration— Abram's offspring will be so vast that they cannot be counted. Only God could present a scenario of this nature to a man already into his eighties. At the human level it is a promise that has no hope of being fulfilled. Once more it challenges Abram to believe God and not merely look at his circumstances.

While Abram is receiving further assurances of God's plans for his future, the same cannot be said of Lot. He begins to discover for himself the folly of living among a degenerate people who are on their way to final judgement by God. The first clear sign of this comes when Lot is captured by a raiding party and he and his whole family are taken away captive. Abram, on nearing the news, sets out in pursuit. He overtakes and defeats the kings who had planned this raid and brings back Lot, together with all his possessions.

This book is not intended to tell the whole history of Israel, but Lot's capture and rescue are significant as they release further prophetic blessings. The first of these comes from Melchizedek, king of Salem, who comes to meet Abram on his return from freeing Lot. Melchizedek declares: *"Blessed be Abram by God Most High, Creator* (and possessor or owner) *of heaven and earth."*[24] This blessing has a twofold significance:

- It acknowledges Abram's relationship with God
- It acknowledges God's ownership of the earth

The lands and the nations are God's to give as he chooses and we need to remember that. As has often been said; 'man proposes, God disposes.'

24   Genesis 14:19

This theme of prophetic blessing is continued throughout Genesis fifteen. The first verse restates God's relationship with Abram: *"Do not be afraid, Abram. I am your shield, your very great reward."*[25] Interestingly, this time Abram does question God. He has come all this way, but his faith is weakening. Maybe he is seeking reassurance. He doesn't berate God, and neither should we, but he does pour out his heart. He is old, he cannot see how he and his wife can have a child—and the promise of God to bless his offspring seems difficult to accept. But God understands his anguish and speaks to him again: *"A son coming from your own body will be your heir."*[26] This statement is fundamental if we are to have a right understanding of the lineage of Jesus and the history of God's promises to Israel. We need to grasp its significance if we want to see who are the legitimate heirs to these covenants.

At this time God also reminds Abram of His previous promise that his offspring will be beyond counting. God takes Abram outside and says to him; *"Look up at the heavens and count the stars—if indeed you can count them. So shall your offspring be."*[27] This is enough for Abram. His heart is stirred by faith once more and the Bible records; *Abram believed the LORD and He credited it to him as righteousness.*[28]

God continues by explaining that it was He who brought Abram out of the Chaldees to *"give you this land to take possession of it."*[29] It is fascinating that Abram, having believed God for his future, had found himself wracked with doubt about the present and how all these things could possibly take place. Yet God knew that weakness (as he knows ours) and, rather than rebuking Abram for asking the question, God demonstrated His commitment to the covenant.

The rest of this amazing chapter presents a full account of the promises God makes to Abram. Given that the Bible deals with matters in their essentials only, this detail should be a

25   Genesis 15:1
26   Genesis 15:4
27   Genesis 15:5
28   Genesis 15:6
29   Genesis 15:7

signal to us of the significance of this covenant.

Firstly, God commands Abram to bring Him a heifer, a goat and a ram, each three years old, along with a dove and a pigeon. You may wonder why Abram then cuts the animals in half and arranges the halves opposite each other with the dove and young pigeon, still whole, laid among them. Is God demanding a sacrifice of atonement before the law? Not in the least.

At that time, a binding agreement was sometimes entered into by killing and dividing an animal and walking amongst the pieces. This symbolised your acceptance of the agreement and also the fate that would await you if you broke the covenant. Abram set out the pieces so that both he, and God, could enter into covenant agreement. God however, had other plans, for He knew the covenant He was proposing was one that, humanly speaking, it would be impossible for Abram to keep.

Abram *fell into a deep sleep, and a thick and dreadful darkness came over him.*[30] The Lord then speaks to him again. *"Know for certain that your descendants will be strangers in a country not their own, and they will be enslaved and ill-treated four hundred years. But I will punish the nations they serve as slaves, and afterwards they will come out with great possessions . . . In the fourth generation your descendants will come back here, for the sin of the Amorites has not yet reached its full measure."*[31]

Here, in this first specific account of what will happen to Abram's family, God warns him there will be four hundred years of slavery and hardship. You might have thought that by now Abram would have been hearing about wine and roses or more appropriately, vines and fig trees! Not the least of it.

There is a mood abroad in the world, which unfortunately finds itself mirrored in many of our church programmes, that wants and expects an instant response or an instant solution.

30   Genesis 15:12
31   Genesis 15:13-14 and 16

We live in a world of mass, express communication and we expect our lives to be resolved in the same way. God was making it clear to Abram that if he followed God's plan for his life, there would be long periods that his descendants might see as harsh and fruitless. But (and it is a very important but!) in the fullness of time God would judge the nations surrounding Israel, and God would keep His promises. The same preparation may apply to us as God refines us and we must look at God's dealings with His people of Israel through His perspective, not ours.

From this passage, with its warnings of future suffering, we move to the covenant God makes with Abram at this time. The sun has set and God causes a smoking brazier with a blazing torch to appear and pass between the pieces. This is a supernatural attestation of the presence of God. You will remember that in Genesis thirteen God had promised Abram all the land that he could see. Now, in order to establish this in context, God spells out the borders of the land, something we will find repeated as we examine Israel's title deeds elsewhere. If the first time the promise was made is like a sketched outline, this is a detailed boundary map.

On that day the LORD made a covenant with Abram and said: "To your descendants I give this land, from the river (or Wadi) *of Egypt to the great river, the Euphrates—the land of the Kenites, Kenizzites, Kadmonites, Hittites, Perizzites, Rephaites, Amorites, Canaanites, Girgashites and Jebusites."*[32]

When God speaks so clearly, it raises questions in people's minds as to why the Israelites should dispossess nations and inhabit their lands. It is an issue that offends many. It disturbs their sense of what they see as fair play. At this stage many Christians begin to decide that not all the Bible is inspired. It is an important issue and one which recurs throughout their history; as such, it cannot be fudged.

32   Genesis 15:18-21

In promising the land of Canaan to Abram and his descendants, God told Abram this would not happen until the sin of the Amorites reached full measure. What God meant by this was that He would only act after the Amorites had repeatedly rejected God and pursued the idols and foreign gods they chose for themselves.

As creator of the earth, God is entitled to distribute land as he chooses, but as a God of justice, this is not done on a whim. Our right to govern or rule over areas of the earth is affected by the sin of our nation and its attitude both towards God and His people. Once again we need to take a long-term view and understand that it is only after repeated failure to acknowledge God that He intervenes in this way.

God has always judged nations and He will continue to do so. If we decide that offends our sense of justice, we are claiming to be wiser than our Creator. The Bible tells us very clearly that at the end of the ages all the peoples of the world will be judged. God's present judgements are a shadow of what is to come in that final day.

The Word of God itself reminds us that, *All scripture is God-breathed and is useful for teaching, rebuking, correcting and training in righteousness, so that the man of God may be thoroughly equipped for every good work.*[33] We cannot impose our view of what God should or should not do, because of our cultural or personal background. The Word of God is either reliable and absolute, or vague and changeable. If it is possible to change the Word of God to suit the mood of the day we are all in deep trouble. If we try to shoehorn God into current thinking, the Word of God, the Bible, becomes disposable. We cease to grasp and understand its importance.

The promise of God's future provision for his family was enough to convince Abram of the Lord's faithfulness, but unfortunately there was one area where he and Sarai really struggled.

33   2 Timothy 3:16-17

When we come to the story of Ishmael, we come face to face again with Abram and Sarai's humanity. Unable to hold onto God's promise that they will bear a child, they try to help God out by coming up with their own solution. Those of us who are Christians have probably all been there—after all, it seemed a good idea at the time! In the case of Abram and Sarai, they began to lose patience as they waited for God to provide Sarai with the promised son. Not wishing to leave themselves without a dynasty, a plan is hatched. Sarai will give her Egyptian maidservant, Hagar, to Abram, so that at least they will have an heir.

> If it is possible to change the Word of God to suit the mood of the day then we are all in deep trouble.

It's a story with puzzling and tragic consequences. Hagar, on becoming pregnant, despises Sarai. As a result Sarai ill-treats Hagar, who runs away with her son, Ishmael. God is not indifferent to Hagar's treatment, and the angel of the Lord meets her. He tells her, *"I will so increase your descendants that they will become too numerous to count."* At the same time he warns; *"He will be a wild donkey of a man; his hand will be against everyone and everyone's hand against him, and he will live in hostility toward all his brothers."*[34] The truth of those prophetic words has echoed down through history to the present day, as we see the current conflicts between Israel and its Arab neighbours.

What was the result of Abram and Sarai trying to arrange things on God's behalf? The answer, in a nutshell, was strife. They thought they could help God, but instead left a legacy of

34   Genesis 16:10 and 12

resentment that has lasted to this day. So often, when we strive in our own strength, that is the result. Abram the patriarch, man of God that he undoubtedly was, still failed.

I have often thought that if you didn't have the witness of the Holy Spirit to the truth of God's Word, common sense would tell you it must be true. After all, no one trying to sell a family as a public relations exercise, would willingly let people know their weakness and mistakes, yet the Bible (and Abram's story in particular) is littered with them. Abram was a man of outstanding faith but he was like you or me in all his weaknesses; all too human. It was to be another thirteen years before Abram was to see the child of the promise, but it was through this child, and not Ishmael, that God would renew the Abrahamic covenants.

Chapter 2

ISAAC'S EARLY YEARS

Now the LORD was gracious to Sarah as He had said, and the LORD did for Sarah what He had promised. Sarah became pregnant and bore a son to Abraham in his old age, at the very time God had promised him . . . Sarah said, "God has brought me laughter, and everyone who hears about this will laugh with me." And she added, "Who would have said to Abraham that Sarah would nurse children? Yet I have borne him a son in his old age."

Genesis 21:1, 2, 6 and 7

Abram has waited and waited for a son. He is now ninety-nine years old. The son of his wife's slave is now thirteen. At this stage, after all these years of waiting, God returns with a reminder of the covenant He has already entered into with Abram: *"I am God Almighty; walk before Me and be blameless. I will confirm My covenant between Me and you and will greatly increase your numbers."*[1]

This time however, God goes further: *"As for Me, this is My covenant with you: You will be the father of many nations. No longer will you be called Abram; your name will be Abraham, for I have made you the father of many nations. I will make you very fruitful; I will make nations of you, and kings will come from you. I will establish My covenant as an everlasting covenant between Me and you and your descendants for the generations to come, to be your God and the God of your descendants after you. The whole land of Canaan, where you are now an alien, I will give as an*

1   Genesis 17:1-2

everlasting possession to you and your descendants after you; and I will be their God."[2]

What do we see from this covenant?

- Firstly, the covenant of fruitfulness is repeated. Abraham will be the father of many nations, as the new name God gives him signifies
- The kingly line, which will produce David and *'great David's greater son'*, Jesus, will be established in the future
- God repeats the promise that Abraham's descendants will inherit the whole land of Canaan
- The land is given through *'an everlasting covenant'* and as *'an everlasting possession.'*

When God declares something to be everlasting, that is simply and absolutely what it becomes. Many problems of interpretation arise because they are just that—our interpretation. The context of all Bible verses we read has to be the whole revealed Word of God. The word used here for everlasting is 'olam', which means ages or, literally, throughout all the ages. God's covenants remain the same throughout the ages. No man and no doctrine emanating from man can change that.

At this time, God repeats his promise to Abraham concerning the son of the promise. He tells Abraham that Sarai's name will now be Sarah. Her new name means princess, one honoured. God tells Abraham that He *"will surely give you a son by her."*[3] Once God has honoured Sarah, He prepares to bless her. It is a striking example of how God's eternal purposes, worked out through our lives, may be many years in preparation.

At this time Abraham, the man of faith, who has heard God renew His promises, bless him and honour Sarah, finds it all too much. He is a hundred, his wife is ninety and he cannot quite believe it anymore. Instead he asks that Ishmael may live under God's blessing. In a limited way we can see a parallel to that of the Church concerning Israel. Christians look at the nation of Israel, seemingly decayed beyond the possibility of redemption and use in God's plans. They see only the Church and cannot believe God still wants to use Israel. Of course God does and will use the Church and of course the Church has a purpose which far outstrips that of Ishmael. But there is a significant purpose that God wants Israel to fulfil and when we try to usurp it we can so easily become Ishmaels. And what does that lead to? It leads to conflict, division and striving. Let's remember that as we look at God's response to Abraham's request.

God's covenants remain the same throughout the ages. No man and no doctrine emanating from man can change that.

Then God said: *"Yes, but your wife Sarah will bear you a son, and you will call him Isaac. I will establish My covenant with him as an everlasting covenant for his descendants after him. And as for Ishmael, I have heard you: I will surely bless him; I will make him fruitful and will greatly increase his numbers. He will be the father of twelve rulers, and I will make him into a great nation. But my covenant I will establish with Isaac, whom Sarah will bear to you by this time next year."*[4]

God again declares His covenants to Abraham's descendants with striking clarity. The covenant God has already established with Abraham is also to be Isaac's, and it is this covenant which God refers to as everlasting. In summary, God promises that:

- Ishmael will be the father of twelve rulers

4   Genesis 17:19-22

- Sarah will bear a son
- Sarah's son will be called Isaac
- Isaac will enter into the everlasting covenant already promised to Abraham
- Isaac's descendants will be included in this everlasting covenant

The disputes that inevitably arise over God's promises to these two children of Abraham (Ishmael and Isaac) happen because we fail to look at scripture. God responds to Abraham's plea and agrees to bless Ishmael, but God chooses to establish His covenant with Sarah's son, Isaac. It is important for us to realise that whatever schemes or arguments man has come up with, God has never changed that promise throughout history.

God repeats His promise that Sarah will bear a son: *Then the Lord said, "I will surely return to you about this time next year, and Sarah your wife will have a son."*[5] This time it is Sarah's turn to be disbelieving and she laughs at what God tells her. God rebukes her gently, but then asks, *"Is anything too hard for the LORD. I will return to you at the appointed time next year and Sarah will have a son."*[6]

What an amazing picture of God's mercy, kindness and patience in the outworking of His purposes. Once again He reminds them that what seems impossible to man is always possible to God. This story should encourage us when our own faith is weak or when we feel that we have let God down—there is always hope for the future. We should remind ourselves of that as we consider both our own lives and the state of the Jewish people in Israel and around the world.

Finally, in Genesis twenty-one, we come to the birth of Isaac. I wonder if we can imagine what this event must have been like. Here, after all these years of being virtually alone in an alien landscape, they finally receive the promise of God for

---

5   Genesis 18:10
6   Genesis 18:14

which they had been waiting. Of course, a major part of the miracle of this birth is in their age. God wanted to demonstrate His supernatural hand to those who lived around them. It was a confirmation of God's special blessing upon them. After all, following the flood a hundred year old father and a ninety year old mother are not exactly commonplace! Following Isaac's birth, Abraham circumcised Isaac on the eighth day, in obedience to everything God had told him to do.

Time passes and as Sarah continues to wean her son Isaac, Ishmael mocks him. One senses he realised what Isaac's birth would mean for his own future and I suspect jealousy had a very real part to play in it all. Like other Bible characters such as King Saul, he is unable to accept his own place in God's plan. It's all too easy for us to mock or undermine others, when we realise they have a role in God's kingdom which might not fall to us. That personal jealousy can so easily find its reflection in our churches and even in our nation.

As for Abraham, his paternal instincts are upset when Sarah begins to demand that Hagar and Ishmael should be sent away. Once again God has to speak clearly to him, to make Abraham understand why this is necessary: *"It is through Isaac that your offspring will be reckoned. I will make the son of the maidservant into a nation also."*[7] Though humanly the separation may seem harsh, God does not want there to be any confusion over whose inheritance it is, but He sends Ishmael away compassionately. He meets with Hagar and Ishmael and tells her: *"I will make him into a great nation."*[8]

In examining these scriptures, we see the promise re-confirmed. It will be through Isaac that Abraham's offspring will be counted, but it is not at the expense of others. The conflicts arise when the sons of the slave woman try to overthrow God's Word and claim the land that belongs

7   Genesis 21:12-13
8   Genesis 21:18

to the descendants of Abraham and Isaac. That conflict is still alive today.

Returning to Isaac, we move on a number of years to the time when as a boy he is leaving childhood. In looking at God's dealings with the patriarchs, we have already noted that we cannot ignore any passages that are difficult or puzzling. In Genesis twenty-two we come to one such passage. God asks Abraham to take Isaac, probably by this time a young man, to the region of Mount Moriah. They have to set out on a journey of some sixty miles, Abraham knowing all the time what God has required of him. There he is to sacrifice Isaac as a burnt offering before God. What sort of God would do this, you say, and why would Abraham be prepared to obey?

Let us deal with Abraham first. While his faith may have wavered on occasions and in his dealings with others (where his wife was concerned), he had always obeyed God. His trust in God had never been disappointed. God had prospered him and fulfilled His promises. If God was to be trusted, sacrificing Isaac (Abraham's pride and joy) was something that Abraham would do with absolute confidence. Obeying God was a pre-requisite for faith. There is no doubt that he had a strong sense of God's eternal purposes. Paul, writing in Hebrews, tells us that *Abraham reasoned that God could raise the dead.*[9] Through the Holy Spirit he understood God was the author of life.

Abraham also understood the provision of burnt offerings made before the Lord. Abel had brought the best of his flock to the Lord; Noah had sacrificed burnt offerings. They showed worship and honour to God—they were costly. This was to be the most costly sacrifice Abraham could bring. It wasn't, as some suggest, a parallel with the sacrifice of children to Molech, a practice Abraham would have found abhorrent. It was undertaken in complete obedience and submission to God.

Why did God require it? Again, I believe God required it to

9   Hebrews 11:19

test whether Abraham's innermost being was able to give everything to God, honouring God beyond all human and emotional ties. Jesus challenged his followers in a similar

---

We cannot restrict God to an earthly timescale that suits our individual purposes, or into which we can cram our earthbound view of God and His character.

---

way in the New Testament when He told them: *"If anyone comes to me and does not hate his father and mother, his wife and children, his brothers and sisters—yes, even his own life—he cannot be My disciple. And anyone who does not carry his cross and follow Me cannot be My disciple."*[10] Now of course that did not mean he wanted them to literally hate their own families; but Jesus was saying that real faith in God means you will honour and serve God before everything and everyone else—family included.

God brings Abraham to the place where the altar is built, the wood laid and his son bound. Abraham takes up his knife to slay his son, but at this moment the angel of the Lord calls to him, telling him not to touch the boy and instead to sacrifice a ram, caught by its horns in a nearby thicket. God Himself has provided the sacrifice in response to Abraham's obedience.

Behind this dramatic human story, we see the symbol of the offering that was to be made when God would offer his only son, Jesus, as Messiah, not only to be slain, but also to descend into hell. God, in this story, is already foreshadowing that sacrifice.

10   Luke 14:26-27

Out of Abraham's amazing act of obedience and trust in God's supernatural abilities, God speaks to him yet again. *"I swear by Myself, declares the LORD, that because you have done this and have not withheld your son, your only son, I will surely bless you and make your descendants as numerous as the stars in the sky and as the sand on the seashore. Your descendants will take possession of the cities of their enemies, and through your offspring all nations on earth will be blessed, because you have obeyed Me."*[11]

Again we note God's emphatic language:

- God's very name is appended to this agreement
- Abraham's descendants will be without number
- Abraham's descendants will dispossess their enemies
- Through Abraham all the nations of the earth will be blessed

We will see later how that was practically fulfilled. Moving out of our historical timeframe for a moment, we can see that there was a New Testament fulfilment of the fourth promise when the early church, scattered throughout the known world by persecution, took with it the gospel of Jesus Christ. God was going to use the obedience of one individual to bring about universal blessing.

Some twelve years after this test of Abraham's faith, his wife Sarah died at the age of a hundred and twenty-seven. Abraham purchased a burial plot for her at Kiriath Arba (present day Hebron). The site and town are spiritually significant. They contain a resting place of the patriarchs; they were a royal city, a city of refuge and a Levitical city. Given their spiritual significance it is little wonder that modern-day Hebron has so often been a place of conflict.

Finally Abraham's life also ends. When Abraham died, at the age of one hundred and seventy-five, he did so in confident assurance that God would honour His Word, but he died

11   Genesis 22:15-18

without seeing the physical fulfilment of that Word. It is an immense challenge for us when we realise that we cannot restrict God to an earthly timescale that suits our individual purposes, or into which we can cram our earthbound view of God and his character. It is a theme which will recur throughout this astonishing story of God's dealings with mankind.

While we will not re-examine all the scriptures we visit, it is good to present a summary of the scriptures we have read in these early Biblical declarations of God's purposes for Israel, for they paint the background to the journey on which God's people will travel:

"I will make you into a great nation and I will bless you; I will make your name great, and you will be a blessing. I will bless those who bless you, and whoever curses you I will curse; and all peoples on earth will be blessed through you"
Genesis 12:2-3

The words that God spoke to Abram after Lot had parted from him:

"Lift up your eyes from where you are and look north and south, east and west. All the land that you see I will give to you and your offspring forever. I will make your offspring like the dust of the earth, so that if anyone could count the dust, then your offspring could be counted. Go, walk through the length and breadth of the land, for I am giving it to you."
Genesis 13:14-17

"Do not be afraid, Abram. I am your shield, your very great reward."
Genesis 15:1

"Your descendants will be strangers in a country not their own, and they will be enslaved and ill-treated four

hundred years. But I will punish the nation they serve and afterwards they will come out with great possessions."

Genesis 15:13-14

On that day the LORD made a covenant with Abram and said, "To your descendants I give this land, from the river (or Wadi) *of Egypt to the great river, the Euphrates—the land of the Kenites, Kenizzites, Kadmonites, Hittites, Perizzites, Rephaites, Amorites, Canaanites, Girgashites and Jebusites."*

Genesis 15:18-21

"I will confirm My covenant between Me and you and will greatly increase your numbers."

Genesis 17:2

God said to (Abram), "As for Me, this is My covenant with you: You will be the father of many nations. No longer will you be called Abram; your name will be Abraham, for I have made you a father of many nations. I will make you very fruitful; I will make nations of you, and kings will come from you. I will establish My covenant as an everlasting covenant between Me and you and your descendants for the generations to come, to be your God and the God of your descendants after you. The whole land of Canaan, where you are now an alien, I will give as an everlasting possession to you and your descendants after you; and I will be their God."

Genesis 17:3-8

"Your wife Sarah will bear you a son, and you will call him Isaac. I will establish My covenant with him as an everlasting covenant for his descendants after him."

Genesis 17:19

"Is anything too hard for the LORD. I will return to you at the appointed time next year and Sarah will have a son."

Genesis 18:14

"It is through Isaac that your offspring will be reckoned."
Genesis 21:12

"I swear by Myself, declares the LORD, *"that because you have done this and have not withheld your son, your only son, I will surely bless you and make your descendants as numerous as the stars in the sky and as the sand on the seashore. Your descendants will take possession of the cities of their enemies, and through your offspring all nations on earth will be blessed, because you have obeyed Me."*
Genesis 22:15-18

The Promises in Summary

- Abraham will be blessed

- His descendants will be blessed

- His son Isaac will be blessed

- Abraham's descendants of the promise will know God's protection

- The whole world will be blessed through his descendants

- Canaan will belong to Abraham's descendants of the covenant—that is, Isaac

- The land and borders are spelt out in detail

- Times of exile and return are predicted

- Those who bless Israel will be blessed

- Those who curse Israel will be cursed

- Ishmael will be a great nation, but the covenant promises are not his

- Ishmael will be in conflict with his brothers

Chapter 3

ISAAC AND JACOB

So they sent their sister Rebekah on her way . . . And they blessed Rebekah and said to her: "Our sister, may you increase to thousands upon thousands; may your offspring possess the gates of their enemies."

Genesis 24:59-60

Abraham is determined that Isaac, miraculously born in Sarah's old age, born because of God's amazing promises, should marry from among his own people. He doesn't want Isaac marrying from among the Canaanites, who don't serve God. Genesis twenty-four tells the fascinating tale of how Isaac comes to marry Rebekah.

Abraham instructs a trusted servant to go to his own people and to find a wife for Isaac from among them. It is another remarkable demonstration of God's detailed provision for His servants. Not knowing how to find a wife for his master's son, the servant who has been sent to Nahor makes a request of God: *"May the girl I ask for water also offer to water the camels."*[1] Before he has finished praying, Rebekah comes along. By divine circumstance, she just happens to be the grand-daughter of Abraham's brother. Faced with a journey to a distant land and marriage to a man she has never seen, she is given a free choice in the matter by her own family. She doesn't hesitate but, taking her maids with her, sets out to meet Isaac. The King James version, in that lovely poetic language for which it is known, finishes the passage with these words; *Isaac brought her into his mother Sarah's tent,*

1 Genesis 24:14 extracted

and took Rebekah, and she became his wife; and he loved her: and Isaac was comforted after his mother's death.[2]

When God sets out through history to achieve something He always goes ahead, preparing a path for what is to happen. Once more, in this wonderful passage of scripture, we see echoes of the preparation for the Messiah, Jesus Christ, and the amazing faith and trust of a young woman in God's plan for her life. We observe the same intimate detail and concern again and again in God's dealing with Israel. More than that, such passages show us God's heart and provision for each one of us. As we are able to understand, appreciate and receive it for ourselves, we know that as we ally ourselves to God's plans and purposes, He is preparing the same comprehensive plans for our lives.

Rebekah and Isaac have no children and so Isaac comes before God and asks that Rebekah will be able to conceive. While the twins are still in the womb, Rebekah can feel them jostling one another, so she asks God what is happening. This is his response; *"Two nations are in your womb, and two people from within you will be separated; one people will be stronger than the other, and the older will serve the younger."*[3] And so the two sons, Esau and Jacob, are born. Esau is a hairy man, a hunter, while Jacob is smooth-skinned and quiet, staying among the tents.

One day, when they are grown men, Esau comes back from hunting, famished and longing for food. He asks Jacob for some stew. Jacob, never slow to seize an opportunity, offers to give him some food in exchange for his birthright and Esau, desperate with hunger, agrees. He doesn't stop to think about the possible repercussions. Genesis twenty-five records the transaction with this comment: *So Esau despised his birthright.*[4] It was to have everlasting consequences. How often do we treat the provision of God in this way? It is a sober warning to us to be careful with the gifts and

2   Genesis 24:67
3   Genesis 25:23
4   Genesis 25:34

privileges we receive from the Lord.

Later, because of a famine, Isaac takes the family to Gerar. His herdsmen quarrel with others over the rights to wells, until finally he comes to Beersheba, where no one disputes his rights. There God meets with him and tells him: *"I am the God of your father Abraham. Do not be afraid, for I am with you; I will bless you and increase the number of your descendants for the sake of My servant Abraham."*[5]

There are four notable strands to this encounter with God:

- God is prepared to personally identify with Abraham
- Increase will come because of the covenant God entered into with Abraham
- Isaac will enter this same blessing
- Isaac does not need to be afraid as God is watching over him

Isaac, aware of the significance of this meeting with God, builds an altar. The altar is a demonstration of freely given worship and is built in thanksgiving for God's promises. It is a practical, external expression of faith and trust in God's Word.

Many years pass and we find Isaac, old and with failing eyesight, thinking about his own mortality and wanting to pass on God's prophetic blessing. Knowing it is Isaac's intention to pass on the blessing to Esau (as the elder son), Rebekah persuades Jacob to pretend to be Esau. She gives him Esau's best clothes to wear, and puts goatskins on his hands and his neck to disguise the smoothness of his skin. She herself makes a tasty meal for Isaac and then gives it to Jacob to take to his father. Unable to see clearly, Isaac is persuaded it must be Esau (though he does express suspicions about his voice). He blesses Jacob with these words: *"May God give you of heaven's dew and of earth's richness—an abundance of grain and new wine. May nations serve you and*

5   Genesis 26:24

peoples bow down to you. Be lord over your brothers, and may the sons of your mother bow down to you. May those who curse you be cursed and those who bless you be blessed."[6]

Esau, who has been out hunting to produce for his father this special meal and receive the blessing, returns too late to uncover this subterfuge. He pleads with Isaac to give him a blessing, but the birthright has already been given. Isaac answers Esau: *"Your dwelling will be away from the earth's richness, away from the dew of the heaven above. You will live by the sword and serve your brother. But when you grow restless you will throw the yoke from off his neck."*[7]

Again, there will be those who say, surely this isn't fair? Jacob has received the birthright blessing by deceit; how can God allow this to happen? There are three reasons why, although we might not condone the deceit, God allowed it. We have already commented on the first: Esau had already sold his birthright for a quick meal. The Bible (as we saw) recounts that Esau despised his birthright. The second is that Esau had already allied himself in marriage to members of Ishmael's family, whereas at this time God was calling on the patriarchs to marry from among their own families, to keep themselves free from foreign gods. The third is that God had already declared, before Jacob's birth, that it would be through his line that the covenant would be kept.

One might add a fourth reason. The Bible says that man looks on the outward appearance, yet God looks on the heart. God is already preparing Jacob for service, even though he is not yet fully aware of it.

Rebekah, realising that Esau now hates Jacob, persuades Isaac to send Jacob away to her brother, Laban. Isaac agrees with the need for Jacob to find a suitable bride and commands him to go, adding this blessing: *"May God Almighty bless you and make you fruitful and increase your numbers until*

6   Genesis 27:28-29
7   Genesis 27:39-40

you become a community of peoples. May He give you and your descendants the blessing given to Abraham, so that you may take possession of the land where you now live as an alien, the land God gave to Abraham."[8]

Once more this prophetic blessing reinforces God's covenant and is specific about those who will be blessed. Isaac refers to God's blessing to Abraham, and he refers specifically to the promise that the land will be theirs as an inheritance. It is clear from this statement, if it were not already abundantly apparent, that those who inherit the blessing are descendants of Jacob, not of Ishmael or Esau.

As Jacob is on his journey, God meets with him. In a dream Jacob sees the Lord and hears Him speak these words: *"I am the LORD, the God of your father Abraham and the God of Isaac. I will give you and your descendants the land on which you are lying. Your descendants will be like the dust of the earth, and you will spread out to the west and to the east, to the north and to the south. All peoples on earth will be blessed through you and your offspring. I am with you and will watch over you wherever you go, and I will bring you back to this land."*[9]

Here God introduces Himself to Jacob with a five-fold promise:

- A declaration that God is his God
- A promise to give Jacob and his offspring the land
- A promise to watch over Jacob
- A prophetic promise that all the earth will be blessed through Jacob
- A promise to be with Jacob wherever he is

God declares that the covenant given to Abraham, and through him to Isaac, now rests on Jacob. The Lord repeats His promise that through Jacob's seed all the peoples of the earth will be blessed, a promise that encompasses not only

8   Genesis 28:3-4
9   Genesis 28:13-15

Israel, but all mankind. Again, echoing down through the ages, we catch a glimpse of the heart of God, resolved not only to bless a man, a family, a tribe, or even a nation, but all mankind.

As has already been stated, it is not the intention of this book to tell the story of the patriarchs in detail, fascinating as it is. When Jacob arrives in the land where he is to live in exile, Laban, Jacob's uncle, proves more than adept in matching him for cunning. Jacob works seven years for Rachel, Laban's younger daughter, but is given Leah, the elder. If Jacob has any doubt about the deceit Uncle Laban would stoop to, he now has no illusions! However, because of his love for Rachel, he agrees to work for seven more years, so that he may have Rachel as his wife. Seven days later, in return for that agreement of seven years more service, she becomes his bride. Once again, woven through the weakness of men's dealings with one another, we find the steadfast purposes of God.

Although the years pass, the relationship between Jacob and Uncle Laban does not improve—if anything it worsens. Deceit is met with deceit, but in everything Jacob does, God blesses him until God intervenes again, instructing Jacob to return to Canaan: *"Go back to the land of your fathers and relatives, and I will be with you."*[10]

As Jacob approaches the land where Esau lives, the angels of God meet him. He prays to God and that night he has a personal encounter with the Lord. His body is touched but more than that, through this personal encounter God touches Jacob's heart and changes his name. From now on, he will no longer be called Jacob (the grasper or deceiver) but Israel— the one who wrestles with God, or who is a prince with God. We would do well to remember the aspect of Jewish behaviour God saw in redeemed Jacob, when we look at the behaviour of many in Israel today.

10   Genesis 31:3

God commands Jacob to go to Bethel (the house of God) and settle there. In obedience Jacob responds, at the same time burying all the foreign gods his family have brought with them. Once more, God speaks with him, telling him: *"Your name is Jacob, but you will no longer be called Jacob; your name will be Israel." So He named him Israel. And God said to him: "I am God Almighty; be fruitful and increase in number. A nation and a community of nations will come from you, and kings will come from your body. The land I gave to Abraham and Isaac I also give to you, and I will give this land to your descendants after you."*[11]

Again, God brings a series of prophetic commands and promises to Jacob:

- Be fruitful (the word used to Adam in the Garden of Eden)
- A nation and community of nations will come from you
- I give this land to you
- I give this land to your descendants after you
- Kings will come from this nation (and ultimately, the King of kings)

The sceptre will not depart from Judah, nor the ruler's staff from between his feet, until He comes to whom it belongs, and the obedience of the nations is His.

In all of this, God proclaims His own authority. It is not a matter open to discussion; this is God the Creator, Almighty

11   Genesis 35:9-12

and Everlasting. God commands a blessing: Israel is to be fruitful and multiply. Once again the land is promised to Israel, as it has been to Abraham and Isaac. Further than that, God looks ahead prophetically and tells Jacob he will be the father of kings. God speaks in unambiguous language of his determined plans for his people, now for the first time known as Israel.

The story of the twelve sons who are born to Jacob make fascinating reading in themselves; competition and jealousy between the sisters, the use of their handmaids to boost their status and standing and God's final response to Rachel's barrenness. Yet though it is Rachel Jacob loves more than any other, it is to Leah, her sister, not the beauty of the family, that God gives the son who will be central to the purpose of God in coming generations. Judah (praise) is her fourth son, the one who finally makes Leah feel vindicated and honoured as a woman. It is the line of Judah we will trace through history, not the line of Rachel's children, even though Joseph's descendants might have seemed the natural choice.

When we read the story of Jacob's sons as they grow up, we are struck at how patient God is with this jealous and squabbling family. The decision of Jacob's brothers to sell their brother Joseph, and their indifference to their father's grief as they continue their deceit, holds us enthralled and amazed. Joseph's eventual rise to become the second-most powerful man in Egypt, his interpretation of Pharaoh's dreams and his brothers' ultimate dependence on him (just as Joseph's childhood dreams had predicted) are well chronicled. What transcends that history, and has eternal significance for Israel, is contained in the blessings given by Jacob, at the time when Joseph has been installed as Pharaoh's right-hand man.

There are two noteworthy elements in these blessings; the first concerns Joseph's sons and the second concerns Judah.

It might have been thought that the promises of God would be fulfilled through Joseph. After all, it is with him God has spoken. Joseph is the one who has been faithful and he is the one who is ultimately responsible for safeguarding the future of the family. Time and again we are led to see that God's thoughts are not our thoughts, nor His ways our ways.

Joseph is indeed blessed by God, but perhaps not in the manner we might have expected. While in Egypt, he has been given a wife, Asenaph, daughter of a priest of On. He names the two sons born to him in Egypt as Manasseh and Ephraim. Manasseh, because God has made him forget his trouble (in other words he recognises how much God has blessed him), and Ephraim, because God has made him fruitful in the land where he is living.

Joseph goes to see his elderly father with his two sons and Jacob tells him: *"Ephraim and Manasseh will be mine, just as Reuben and Simeon are mine."*[12] From this time on they will be reckoned in the future tribal inheritance. In the preceding two verses Jacob has reminded Joseph of God's promise: *"I am going to make you fruitful and will increase your numbers. I will make you a community of peoples, and I will give this land as an everlasting possession to your descendants after you."*[13] Jacob links Joseph's two sons, not only with his own blessing and inheritance, but with God's promise for the tribes who will inherit the land *'as an everlasting possession.'*

Again, some may wonder why those not born of pure descent should be included in these promises. I have no doubt that Joseph and his wife, whatever her previous background, worshipped God. The names of the children tell us that, the way God blessed Joseph tell us that; and the words God spoke prophetically through Jacob confirm that. When Jacob blesses Joseph he asks that God would bless the boys, adding, *"May they be called by my name (Israel) and the names of my*

12   Genesis 48:5
13   Genesis 48:3-4

fathers Abraham and Isaac, and may they increase greatly upon the earth."[14] He also blesses the boys, placing the younger before the firstborn and saying, *"In your name will Israel pronounce this blessing: may God make you like Ephraim and Manasseh."*[15]

As we come to the death of Jacob we see the second significant blessing, central as far as our study is concerned; the blessing given to Judah. *"Judah, your brothers will praise you; your hand will be on the neck of your enemies; your father's sons will bow down to you. You are a lion's cub, O Judah; you return from the prey, my son. Like a lion he crouches and lies down, like a lioness, who dares to rouse him? The sceptre will not depart from Judah, nor the ruler's staff from between his feet, until He comes to whom it belongs, and the obedience of the nations is His. He will tether His donkey to a vine, His colt to the choicest branch; He will wash His garments in wine, His robes in the blood of grapes. His eyes will be darker than wine, His teeth whiter than milk."*[16]

From these verses we note that:

- Judah is to be the chief among the tribes
- A line of rulers will come from Judah
- The Messiah will come from Judah

This passage contains a prophetic vision of Judah's future role in Israel's history. From Judah's line of kings will eventually come a king to whom all the nations will have to bow. It is good to remind ourselves that while the first part of this prophetic message has come to pass, the nations still have to come before Jesus as their king. Are we ready and prepared for that time?

14   Genesis 48:16
15   Genesis 48:20
16   Genesis 49:8-12

A Summary of God's Promises
to Jacob (Israel)

*"May God give you of heaven's dew and of earth's richness—
an abundance of grain and new wine. May nations serve you
and peoples bow down to you. Be lord over your brothers,
and may the sons of your mother bow down to you. May those
who curse you be cursed and those who bless you be blessed."*

Genesis 27:28-29

*"May God Almighty bless you and make you fruitful and
increase your numbers until you become a community of
peoples. May He give you and your descendants the blessing
given to Abraham, so that you may take possession of the
land where you now live as an alien, the land God gave to
Abraham."*

Genesis 28:3-4

*"I am the Lord, the God of your father Abraham and the God
of Isaac. I will give you and your descendants the land on
which you are lying. Your descendants will be like the dust of
the earth, and you will spread out to the west and to the east,
to the north and to the south. All peoples on earth will be
blessed through you and your offspring. I am with you and
will watch over you wherever you go, and I will bring you
back to this land."*

Genesis 28:13-15

*The Lord said to Jacob: "Go back to the land of your fathers
and relatives, and I will be with you."*

Genesis 31:3

*"Your name is Jacob, but you will no longer be called Jacob;
your name will be Israel." So He named him Israel. And God
said to him: "I am God Almighty; be fruitful and increase in*

number. A nation and a community of nations will come from you, and kings will come from your body. The land I gave to Abraham and Isaac I also give to you, and I will give this land to your descendants after you."

Genesis 35:9-12

In much the same way that the three cords of the Godhead (Father, Son and Holy Spirit) confirm the authority of God's Word, so the Lord's use of the threefold cord of the patriarchs (Abraham, Isaac and Jacob) establishes and confirms the three strands of the eternal covenant:

- A physical promise of land and inheritance
- A promise for the nation
- A promise for the nations of the world

If we are to understand the fullness of God's covenant promise for the nations, which is new life in Christ Jesus, we can only do so if we acknowledge the truth of God's promises to the people of Israel and their right to the land of Israel. It is to those aspects of Israel's history we now turn.

Chapter 4

THE EXODUS FROM EGYPT

Afterwards Moses and Aaron went to Pharaoh and said, "This is what the LORD, the God of Israel, says: "Let My people go, so that they may hold a festival to Me in the desert." Pharaoh said, "Who is the LORD, that I should obey Him and let Israel go? I do not know the Lord and I will not let Israel go."

Exodus 5:1-2

We move on now, some four hundred years. The seventy members of the household that came to Egypt are now a community numbering some 2,000,000. God has indeed made them fruitful! Not all is well however.

As God has foretold, the Egyptians have enslaved Israel. Now, worried by the increasing numbers of these Hebrew slaves, Pharaoh is trying to kill all the male children born to them (much as Herod would do when he heard news of the birth of Jesus). Moses, hidden by his mother in the bulrushes in a desperate attempt to avoid the edict of Pharaoh, has been rescued, ironically by Pharaoh's daughter. He has been brought up with all the privileges and education of a member of the royal household. However, in a fit of temper and misplaced zeal, Moses has killed an Egyptian who was mistreating some Hebrew workers. When Pharaoh hears of it, Moses has to flee Egypt in fear of his life.

A further forty years pass. Moses has met and been accepted

by Jethro, a priest to the Midianites; he is married to one of Jethro's daughters and Egypt and its people must seem a lifetime away. All that is changed in one day when Moses meets God, as he goes to examine the phenomenon of a burning bush. Moses' introduction to the Lord is again significant. God declares: *"I am the God of your father, the God of Abraham, the God of Isaac and the God of Jacob."*[1] Even here, in these opening verses, the line of descent is being clearly spelt out—the promise comes through Abraham, Isaac and Jacob.

God explains He has chosen Moses to bring the Israelites out of Egypt. When God tells Moses how he is to do it, standing before Pharaoh and demanding freedom for his people, Moses is understandably nervous of how he will be received. God tells Moses: *"I AM WHO I AM. This is what you are to say to the Israelites: 'I AM has sent me to you.'"*God continues: *"Say to the Israelites, 'The LORD, the God of your fathers—the God of Abraham, the God of Isaac and the God of Jacob—has sent me to you.' This is My Name for ever, the Name by which I am to be remembered from generation to generation."*[2]

The message is repeated in the following verse before God explains: *"I have promised to bring you . . . into the land of the Canaanites, Hittites, Amorites, Perizzites, Hivites and Jebusites—a land flowing with milk and honey."*[3]

Moses has encountered a covenant-keeping God. Firstly, in using the term *"I AM WHO I AM,"* God declares the eternal aspect of His nature and His Kingdom. It has past, present and future meaning. In other words, it is utterly reliable. Twice more God repeats the covenant He has made with Abraham, Isaac and Jacob, reinforcing this with the expression He uses in verse eighteen, describing Himself as *"the God of the Hebrews."* Yet once more He makes it clear where the land is to be, for the first time adding a descriptor: *a land flowing with milk and honey.*

The use of the expression *milk and honey* is no accident. It speaks of a land capable of sustaining herds, but not yet fully cultivated. It is the vine and the fig tree that express full fruitfulness. The children of Israel are to be given an inheritance of land and God will bless that inheritance as they continue to seek God and to listen to Him—nevertheless they will have to work to cultivate it. There's a message there for us. When God calls us, we should remember that He will often expect us to work to cultivate the promise and the opportunities God is giving us, in order to make them what God really intends.

When Moses returns to the land, things appear to become worse. God is aware that Moses' faith needs reinforcing and in the opening verses of Exodus six God delivers an emphatic declaration of His sovereignty and His intent towards the children of Israel. God tells Moses: *"I am the LORD. I appeared to Abraham, to Isaac and to Jacob as God Almighty, but by My Name the LORD I did not make Myself known to them. I also established My covenant with them to give them the land of Canaan, where they lived as aliens . . . I am the LORD . . . I will redeem you . . . I will take you as My own people and I will be your God . . . And I will bring you into the land I swore with uplifted hand to give to Abraham, to Isaac and to Jacob. I will give it to you as a possession. I am the LORD."*[4]

What reassurance Moses must have found in these promises:

- I am the Lord
- I appeared to the Patriarchs
- I have established My covenant over Canaan
- I will give you the land
- I will redeem you
- I come to you not only as God Almighty but as the Lord

What emphasis, what pre-determined purpose!

Once again we find God holding himself, if one may say that

4   Exodus 6:2-8 extracted

reverently, to His binding contract. Four times now He has referred to the promises He has made to the patriarchs (Abraham, Isaac and Jacob). He reminds Moses that He has sworn all this by His Holy Name. He declares again that the land will be theirs. Both here, and in Genesis forty-six, the tribal lines of descent and right to be included are once again clearly outlined.

When we read the story of the ten plagues that befell Egypt and the Egyptians, it's easy, with the benefit of hindsight, to shake our heads at the doubts that assailed Moses at this time and to wonder why he needed such reassurance from God. But faced with a grumbling and ambivalent people, confronted by a powerful king in Pharaoh, surrounded by a court circle of magicians who knew how to conjure up powerful spirits, it's no wonder that Moses must have questioned the outcome. The difference between the real spiritual and physical conflict he faced and the spiritual conflict we may face, is that he pursued God's promises despite the circumstances. So often we lose out on final victory because in the conflict we begin to question and lose faith, once more allowing that siren voice to ask, 'Has God said?'

Pharaoh resists Moses and resists God. Finally, Moses warns Pharaoh that if he refuses to let the people go, all the firstborn in Egypt will be killed. God gives command that each Jewish family is to take a young lamb into their home, kill it and sprinkle the blood on the doorpost and the lintel, so that when the angel of the Lord comes by, they and their household will be safe.

Once more scripture looks forward to the time when one man, Jesus Christ, will become the Passover Lamb for all who believe and once more we see how the children of Israel become a symbol of God's desire to touch and save everyone who believes.

After this devastating plague has swept through the land, Pharaoh sends Moses and the children of Israel from Egypt.

When they have finally escaped through the Red Sea and seen Pharaoh's pursuing army overwhelmed by the waters (surely one of the greatest miracles ever seen) Moses records these words: *"In Your unfailing love You will lead the people You have redeemed. In Your strength You will guide them to Your Holy dwelling . . . You will bring them in and plant them on the mountain of Your inheritance—the place, O LORD, You made for Your dwelling, the sanctuary, O LORD, Your hands established. The LORD will reign for ever and ever."*[5]

The children of Israel celebrate their deliverance in the song of Moses and Miriam. They recognise, through this miraculous escape, that it is the Lord who will give them the land. Moses' words in Exodus fifteen reveal that the area they are to inhabit is significant, not only for Israel, but for the Lord. It is referred to as:

- God's dwelling
- God's sanctuary
- The mountain of God's inheritance

With this threefold declaration, God yet again emphasises the land's importance and His personal involvement in the nation to whom it is given.

Three months after the children of Israel leave Egypt, God comes to Moses and tells him: *"Now if you obey Me fully and keep My covenant, then out of all the nations you will be My treasured possession. Although the whole earth is Mine, you will be for Me a kingdom of priests and a holy nation."*[6]

"I will establish your borders from the Red Sea to the Sea of the Philistines (the Mediterranean) *and from the desert to the River* (Euphrates). *I will hand over to you the people who live in the land and you will drive them out before you."*[7]

However, the children of Israel seem incapable of keeping their side of this agreement. In Genesis thirty-two we see God's anger with the people for so easily deserting Him. He

5   Exodus 15:13,17 and 18
6   Exodus 19:5-6
7   Exodus 23:31

tells Moses that He will wipe them out and make of Moses a great nation, but Moses says to God, *"Remember Your servants Abraham, Isaac and Israel, to whom You swore by Your own self: 'I will make your descendants as numerous as the stars in the sky and I will give your descendants all this land I promised them, and it will be their inheritance forever.'"* [8]

> # Truth is found in God and God's truth needs to be our starting point when we start to ask what should happen in the Middle East.

This dialogue highlights a central and consistent theme in God's dealings with Israel. It illustrates the tension between judgement and mercy, promise and punishment. What God has said He will do, necessarily comes to pass. Moses reminds God of His promises. God accepts the binding condition of His own words. He has sworn by his oath and He will keep His Word. Nonetheless, those who disregard God's warnings cannot expect to escape the consequence of their actions. Justice and mercy are the twin pillars of God's dealings with Israel. They recur again and again as we continue with the story of the nation of Israel.

An early (and bizarre) abandonment of God takes place at the very time Moses is receiving the Ten Commandments from the Lord. From being awestruck and fearful of God's presence on the mountain, within a matter of days the Israelites become convinced Moses is not going to return and so they make a golden calf. As they worship it, they declare that these are the gods that brought them up out of Egypt.

8   Exodus 32:13

When Moses and Joshua finally come down the mountain, they find wild celebrations going on. Furiously, Moses throws down the stone tablets, breaking them. The Levites, stung into action by the re-appearance of their leader, Moses, kill many of the revellers and a plague from God swiftly follows. Furthermore, God tells Moses: *"Go up to the land I promised on oath to Abraham, Isaac and Jacob . . . I will send an angel before you . . . But I will not go with you."*[9] God is still committed to His promises, but angered by the sin of the people He tells Moses He will not go with them.

Moses pleads before God; *"If you are pleased with me, teach me Your ways so I may know You and continue to find favour with You. Remember that this nation is Your people."*[10] Moved by Moses' prayer, humility and desire to serve Him, God reveals Himself to Moses. When He does so, passing by the cleft of the rock where Moses is hidden, God declares His nature in these wonderful verses: *"The LORD, The LORD, the compassionate and gracious God, slow to anger, abounding in love and faithfulness, maintaining love to thousands, and forgiving wickedness, rebellion and sin. Yet He does not leave the guilty unpunished; He punishes the children and their children for the sins of their fathers to the third and fourth generation."*[11]

What a wonderful description of the heart of God we find here. He is:

- Compassionate
- Gracious
- Slow to anger
- Abounding in love
- Faithful
- Constant in love
- Forgiving of wickedness, rebellion and sin

For those who persist in sin there will be punishment, but the

9   Exodus 33:1-3 extracted
10 Exodus 33:13
11 Exodus 34:6-7

heart and nature of God are revealed in the opening phrases of these scriptures. In Ezekiel God declares that He takes no pleasure in the death of the wicked.[12] As God reveals Himself to Moses and through him to the children of Israel, He declares that same divine nature we have seen since the Garden of Eden, a nature longing to restore man to the communion God intended for Him. Forgiving, slow to anger, abounding in love and faithfulness, compassionate and gracious. Yes, sin must be dealt with, but at the heart of this message is redemption, pointing us again towards the Messiah and God's desire for all mankind.

The Law that will be given through Moses is to be a constant reminder to the children of Israel of their own sinful nature. The sacrifices required will be a reminder of the consequences and cost of sin, but they are also another signpost of God's grace, reflecting a time when God Himself will provide a perfect sacrifice, once for all time, for all mankind.

Leaving Exodus behind, we move on to look briefly at further extracts from the scriptures known as the Books of the Law or the Books of Moses. In the penultimate chapter of Leviticus we find God's rewards for obedience and His warnings of punishment if the people desert Him. God states that continued disobedience will lead to the Israelites being scattered among the nations. When this happens their hearts will be made fearful and they will waste away. But this is not the note on which the chapter finishes, for the Lord continues, *"Yet in spite of this, when they are in the land of their enemies, I will not reject them or abhor them so as to destroy them completely, breaking My covenant with them. I am the LORD their God. But for their sake I will remember the covenant with their ancestors whom I brought out of Egypt in the sight of their enemies to be their God. I am the LORD."*[13]

This is a vital, underlying principle in our understanding and

---

12   Ezekiel 18:23
13   Leviticus 26:44-45

examination of Israel. Sin will bring punishment; it may well bring banishment and destruction, but through all of this God will still remember His covenants, because He is faithful to His Word. That principle needs to remain in our minds whenever we consider Israel—past, present and future.

The generation of Israelites Moses brought out of Egypt remain an enigma. While their own children would eventually enter the land of Canaan, they were destined to wander in the wilderness for forty years until they had all died (with the exception of Caleb and Joshua). Despite the amazing miracles that God showed them, despite the daily provision of manna, despite the cloud by day and the pillar of fire by night, this generation of the Jewish nation refused to see the good that God intended for them and spent most of their time grumbling.

I can't help but think, as I read through these chapters, how alike so much of our church life that is. We grumble at God's provision, we grumble against our leaders, we want to do things our own way and we don't want to support anything that hasn't originated in the congregation. It is a form of democracy that God knows nothing of, and it paralyses and kills works of God. Tragically, along the way, many good men are disillusioned and disappointed because they are faced with reluctant, grumbling and malcontented people. We need to change the way we think.

Israel's continued grumbling and their refusal to believe the reports of Caleb and Joshua, result in God barring the whole generation from entering the land. Despite their discontent, and despite the repeated sin of this generation, God has not finished with Israel and He begins preparation for the next generation to enter the land of Canaan, by giving them victories in their battles with the nations around them.

One of the neighbouring kings, Balak (King of Moab) summons a seer by the name of Balaam, in order to place a curse on the Israelites. As a man who made his living through such things, placing a curse like this should have been easy, but Balaam finds he is faced with the Lord Himself, who speaks to him, warning him not to say anything, good or bad. Later Balaam comes to a sticky end, and on this occasion he finds himself unable to tell Balak anything other than the words God gives him. *"God is not a man, that He should lie, nor a son of man, that He should change His mind. Does He speak and not act? Does He promise and not fulfil? I have received a command to bless; He has blessed, and I cannot change it."*[14]

Note the five aspects of God's nature revealed through this passage:

- God is incapable of lying
- God does not change His mind
- When God speaks He acts
- When God promises something He fulfils that promise
- When God blesses, man cannot change it

In other words, Balaam is telling Balak that if God is involved in something it is sheer foolishness to try to oppose it. Yet throughout history there have been those who do not understand that the promises of God to Israel cannot be revoked or changed, whatever so-called enlightened age we believe we live in. Truth is found in God and God's truth needs to be our starting point when we start to ask what should happen in the Middle East. That principle is firmly repeated in Numbers twenty-four where again we read the words: *"May those who bless you be blessed and those who curse you be cursed!"*[15]

The Israelites, the people Balak was so anxious to prevent living among them, are still not in the promised land, but in the closing chapters of Numbers, and the opening chapters of Deuteronomy, we find the borders of the land restated as a

---

14   Numbers 23:19-20
15   Numbers 24:9

reminder of what their inheritance will be.

Firstly, we see that the tribes of Gad and Reuben are given the land of Gilead *"as their possession"*[16] provided they conquer the land of Canaan with the other tribes. Then in chapter thirty-four, we read of the borders of Canaan allotted *'as an inheritance.'*[17] The exact allocation is given in the subsequent verses:

What Scripture unerringly shows, presented in context, is that while God laid blessings and curses before His people, He also laid before them an everlasting covenant that could not be broken.

" 'Your southern side will include some of the desert of Zin along the border of Edom. On the east, your southern boundary will start from the end of the Salt Sea (Dead Sea), *cross south of Scorpion Pass, continue on to Zin and go south of Kadesh Barnea. Then it will go to Hazar Addar and over to Azmon, where it will turn, join the Wadi of Egypt and end at the Sea* (The Mediterranean). *Your western boundary will be the coast of the Great Sea. This will be your boundary on the west. For your northern boundary, run a line from the Great Sea to Mount Hor and from Mount Hor to Lebo Hamath. Then the boundary will go to Zedad, continue to Ziphron and end at Hazar Enan. This will be your boundary to the north.*

For your eastern boundary, run a line from Hazar Enan to Shepham. The boundary will go down from Sepham to Riblah

---

16   Numbers 32:29
17   Numbers 34:2

on the east side of Ain and continue along the slopes east of the Sea of Kinnereth (Galilee). *Then the boundary will go down along the Jordan and end at the Salt Sea.*

This will be your land, with its boundaries on every side.' [18]

God's title deeds are written and published!

What then of the territory East of Jordan? As we come to the book of Deuteronomy, we find it described in chapter three. Moses, speaking to the tribes, declares: *I gave the Reubenites and Gadites the territory north of Aroer by the Arnon Gorge, including half the hill country of Gilead and also all of Bashan, the kingdom of Og, I gave to the half-tribe of Manasseh. And I gave Gilead to Makir. But to the Reubenites and Gadites I gave the territory extending from Gilead down to the Arnon Gorge (the middle of the gorge being the border) and out to the Jabbok River, which is the border of the Ammonites. Its western border was the Jordan in the Arabah, from Kinnereth to the Sea of the Arabah (the Salt Sea), below the slopes of Pisgah.* [19]

Why are these borders restated, and why will we find them restated yet again? As God's promises to the patriarchs are repeated so that there can be no doubt over their validity, so it is with the land. Not only that, but we should understand that God has never revoked that promise, anymore than He has revoked the promises that are theirs through the patriarchs. It is important to remember this when people talk of the land of Palestine as though Israel should not exist, or of the rights of Palestinians to have a state, including part of Jerusalem.

No sooner have we finished this blueprint for the division of the land, than Moses turns to the prophetic inevitability of future generations of the Israelites neglecting the Lord. In Deuteronomy chapter four he warns the people that if they abandon God He will scatter them among the nations.

---

18 Numbers 34:3-12
19 Deuteronomy 3:12-13 and 15-17

However, he goes on to say: *"When you are in distress and all these things have happened to you, then in later days you will return to the LORD your God and obey Him. For the LORD your God is a merciful God; He will not abandon you or destroy you or forget the covenant with your forefathers, which He confirmed to them by oath."*[20] What a summary of God's dealings with His people.

I wonder if any of those there (Moses apart) had any real idea of the tragedy and history of the nation of Israel encapsulated in those few sentences? Disobedience would see the destruction of the state, the scattering of the people among the nations, and the inability of those generations to believe that evil would really fall upon them. But that is not to be the end of the story, for we are brought back again to the 'and yet' of God. God will not forsake them completely. God has sworn an oath, therefore:

- They will never be abandoned
- They will never be destroyed
- They will always be a people of God's covenant with the patriarchs

Again and again we find God reinforcing and declaring the permanence of his promise to His people. Moses wants the people to be in no doubt about this. Having declared the way in which God has revealed Himself to Israel *by testings, by miraculous signs and wonders, by war, by a mighty hand and an outstretched arm, and by great and awesome deeds.*[21] Moses urges the people to follow God so that they may have long lives *in the land the LORD your God gives you for all time.*[22]

In Deuteronomy chapter seven Moses tells the people: *The LORD did not set His affection on you and choose you because you were more numerous than other peoples, for you were the fewest of all peoples. But it was because the LORD loved you and kept the oath He swore to your forefathers that He . . .*

20   Deuteronomy 4:30
21   Deuteronomy 4:34
22   Deuteronomy 4:40

redeemed you from . . . slavery. Know therefore that the LORD your God is God; He is the faithful God, keeping His love to a thousand generations of those that love Him and keep His commands.[23]

It's tempting at this stage to say what a wonderful people the Jews must be to be blessed in this way, but in chapter nine Moses puts them right with a few home truths: *It is not because of your righteousness or your integrity that you are going in to take possession of their land; but on account of the wickedness of these nations.*[24]

Having explained that God is giving them the land *to accomplish what He swore to your fathers, Abraham, Isaac and Jacob* Moses continues in the next verse: *Understand then, it is not because of your righteousness that the Lord your God is giving you this good land to possess, for you are a stiff-necked people.*[25] This brutal appraisal of their own merit demonstrates God's grace to Israel even more vividly. The Lord's watchfulness over Israel is dependent upon His covenant-keeping nature—as is our own individual salvation.

And how does God view the land itself, the inheritance He is giving them? Deuteronomy eleven tells us: *It is a land the LORD your God cares for; the eyes of the LORD your God are continually on it from the beginning of the year to its end.*[26]

However, although we want to see what God's eternal promises are to His people Israel, we cannot ignore God's severe warnings to this same nation. We have already seen and read some of those. We need now to consider Moses' words at the end of Deuteronomy. Moses looks forward through history and sees the children of Israel wandering from God. Speaking prophetically to the coming generations he pleads: *Remember the days of old; consider the generations long past . . . When the Most High gave the nations their inheritance, when He divided all mankind, He set up boundaries for the peoples according to the number of*

23   Deuteronomy 7:7-9
24   Deuteronomy 9:5
25   Deuteronomy 9:6
26   Deuteronomy 11:12

the sons of Israel. For the Lord's portion is His people, Jacob His allotted inheritance.[27] Well, you might say, there's no warning there, these are just wonderful promises.

Again we are drawn to the emphatic language; the centrality of Israel in God's purposes for all mankind—something of which we need to remind ourselves. This is a very personal relationship; they are His people. But we cannot be selective in our use of scripture. As we continue through chapter thirty-two we see that Moses goes on to talk of a people who: *abandoned the God who made them and rejected the Rock of their salvation. They sacrificed to demons . . .* You *deserted the Rock . . . forgot the God who gave you birth . . . The LORD saw this and You rejected them.*[28]

There then follows a heart-sinking catalogue of the disasters that will overtake Israel, a nation referred to as *"without sense."* Tragedy after tragedy will sweep over them, as they fail to listen to the warnings of the prophets and the preachers and yet—*The LORD will judge His people and have compassion on His servants when He sees their strength is gone . . . Rejoice, O nations, with His people, for He will avenge the blood of His servants; He will take vengeance on his enemies and make atonement for His land and people.*[29]

So the people who have rejected the Rock as Saviour (surely another reference to the Messiah), will finally find atonement before the Lord.

Our problem is that, once again, we are inclined to bring our prejudices and preconceptions to scripture in order to make it fit our desired pattern. We want to limit or extend the mercy of God, depending upon our own grasp of what is good, right and fair. Scripture presented in context unerringly shows that while God laid blessings and curses before His people, He also laid before them an everlasting covenant that could not be broken. We would have to conclude from all that all we have read from these opening books of the Law, that Israel's

27 Deuteronomy 32:7-9
28 Deuteronomy 32:15-19 extracted
29 Deuteronomy 32:36 and 43

inalienable rights to the land and a relationship with God, have past, present and future validity.

Chapter 5

JOSHUA LEADS THE TRIBES INTO CANAAN

The LORD said to Joshua son of Nun, Moses' assistant: "Moses My servant is dead. Now then, you and all these people, get ready to cross the Jordan River into the land I am about to give to them—to the Israelites. I will give you every place where you set your foot, as I promised Moses."

Joshua 1:1-3

With the death of Moses, the leadership of the tribes passes to Joshua, the man who for so many years has been at Moses right hand. A series of battles follow, and king by king the local tribes are defeated and the Israelites begin to spread out across the land.

If Genesis and Exodus are specific in their outline of the land Abraham's descendants are to inhabit, Joshua, with its depth of detail, leaves no doubt as to the division and boundaries for all Israel. It is absolutely clear, from a reading of Joshua, that God is determined there will be no room for argument—not least among the tribes themselves!

A first reading of chapters fifteen to twenty-one, with their detailed lists of towns and villages, may initially seem indecipherable, but these chapters are not there by accident. Part of chapter fifteen (taken from the Revised Bible) will illustrate this point.

And the lot for the tribe of the children of Judah according to their families was unto the borders of Edom, even to the wilderness of Zin southwards, at the uttermost part of the south. And their south border was from the uttermost part of the Salt Sea, from the bay that looked southward: And it went out southward of the ascent of Akrabbin, and passed along to Zin, and went by the south of Kadesh Barnea, and passed along by Hezron, and went up to Addar, and turned about to Karka: And it passed along to Azmon, and went out at the brook of Egypt; and the goings out of the border were at the sea: this shall be your south border. And the east border was the Salt Sea, even unto the end of Jordan. And the border of the north quarter was from the bay of the sea at the end of the Jordan; and the border went up to Beth-Hoglah, and passed along by the north of Beth-Arabah; and the border went up to the stone of Bothan the son of Reuben: and the border went up to Debir from the valley of Achor, and so northwards, looking towards Gilgal, that is over against the ascent of Adummim, which is on the south side of the river: and the border passed along to the waters of En-Shemesh, and the goings out thereof were at En-Rogel: And the border went up by the valley of the son of Hinnon unto the side of the Jebusite southward (the same is Jerusalem): and the border went up to the top of the mountain that lieth before the valley of Hinnom westward, which is at the uttermost part of the Rephaim northward: And the border was drawn from the top of the mountain unto the fountain of the waters of Nephtaoth, and went out at the cities of Mount Ephron: and the border was drawn from Baalah (the same is Kiriath-Jearim): And the border turned about from Baalah westward unto Mount Seir and passed along unto the side of Mount Jearim on the north (the same is Chesalon), and went down to Bethshemmesh, and passed along by Timnah: and the border went out unto the side of Ekron northward: and the border was drawn to Shikkeron, and passed along to Mount Baalah, and went out at Jabneel; and the goings out of the border were at the sea.

And the west border was to the Great Sea and the border thereof. This is the border of the children of Judah round about according to their families.

And unto Caleb son of Jephunneh he gave a portion among the children of Judah, according to the command of the Lord to Joshua, even Kiriath-Arba, which Arba was the father of Anak (the same is Hebron). And Caleb drove out thence the three sons of Anak; Sheshai and Ahiman and Talmai, the children of Anak. And he went up thence against the inhabitants of Debir: now the name of Debir beforetime was Kiriath-Sepher. And Caleb said, "He that smiteth Kirath-Sepher and taketh it, to him will I give Achsah my daughter to wife. And Othniel the son of Kenaz, the brother of Caleb, took it: and he gave him Achsah his daughter to wife. And it came to pass, when she came unto him, that she moved him to ask of her father a field: and she lighted down from off her ass; and Caleb said unto her, "What wouldst thou?" And she said, "Give me a blessing; for that thou hast set me in the land of the south, give me also springs of water." And he gave her the upper springs and the nether springs.[1]

What a detailed and colourful picture this would have painted to anyone who knew the land. What wonderful clues to the future kingship of David and from him, of course, the ancestry that stretches to Jesus. Here, in this microcosm of the inheritance of Judah, we find Jerusalem, the future capital of Israel. Here we find Caleb, the other remaining faithful member of a previous generation, conquering Hebron, the city with threefold significance in Israel. Nor is this a whim, the city has been set aside for Caleb *according to the command God gave Joshua.*[2] And here too we find wonderful personal detail of the provision that is made for Caleb's daughter and her husband, provision that includes springs of water. God is directly concerned with the individual as well as with the tribal and national picture. The

---

1   Joshua 15:1-19
2   Joshua 15:13

message is one we can take with us as we look down the centuries to the coming of Christ, demonstrating God's love for each individual in the sacrifice at Calvary.

The passage is only a part of the detailed outline of Judah's inheritance. That includes a list of a hundred cities they

---

So the LORD *gave Israel all the land He had sworn to their forefathers, and they took possession of it and settled there . . . Not one of all the* LORD's *good promises to the House of Israel failed; every one was fulfilled.*

---

inhabited. Reading these words again, thousands of years later, we can see the importance God attached to recording Israel's physical boundaries, boundaries that are as detailed for the other tribes in the chapters that follow.

There was to be no doubt about the land or about the boundaries for the tribes. On the basis of what we read in Joshua chapters fifteen to twenty-one, there should be no room for confusion in our minds. Despite the imposition of United Nations mandates and the plans of nations, God has still ordained that this land belongs to the Jewish nation.

Joshua chapter twenty-one records: *So the* LORD *gave Israel all the land He had sworn to their forefathers, and they took possession of it and settled there . . . Not one of all the* LORD's *good promises to the House of Israel failed; every one was fulfilled.* [3]

When we look at God's promises, past, present and future, we

---

3   Joshua 21:43 and 45

need to recognise that every historical promise God made has been exactly fulfilled. Even if we don't have spiritual understanding, logic would therefore suggest that the promises of God that apply to the future will all come to pass. When faced with that reality, our perspective on the present ownership of the land changes. We may have to wait to see a fulfilment of what God has promised, but in God's time it will happen.

As Joshua came towards the end of his life, he, like Moses before him, laid down a challenge to the people he had led to victory and to their children. In renewing their covenant before God, he urged them to get rid of all the foreign gods there were still among them and to serve God *"with all faithfulness . . . But if serving the LORD seems undesirable to you, then choose for yourselves this day whom you will serve . . . But as for me and my household, we will serve the LORD."*[4] The uneven response of their children and their children's children to this renewed covenant with the Lord, would lead to an uneven and unstable period of history for the tribes of Israel.

---

4   Joshua 24:14-15

Chapter 6

JUDGES, PROPHETS AND A FALLEN KING

The people served the LORD throughout the lifetime of Joshua and of the elders who outlived him . . . After that whole generation had been gathered to their fathers, another generation grew up, who knew neither the LORD nor what He had done for Israel . . . They forsook the LORD, the God of their fathers, who had brought them out of Egypt.

Judges 2:7,10 and 12

It's very easy, when setting out what God has to say about Israel at particular times in her past, to either overstate or ignore God's warnings about the consequences of their actions. As we examine the next stage in their history, covering some three hundred years, we can see how their love for God is like a yo-yo, up and down, remembered and then forgotten. We do so, of course, with the benefit of hindsight and the passage of history, but when we consider our own lives and our walk with God, we begin to realise our own walk often lacks the consistency for which God is longing.

Joshua had reminded the people of all that God had done for them. God, *"gave you a land on which you did not toil and cities you did not build; and you live in them and eat from vineyards and olive groves that you did not plant."*[1] Again however, the promise has already been ringed with a caveat, found in the previous chapter. Joshua warned them: *"be very careful to love the LORD your God . . . If you violate the*

1 Joshua 24:13

*covenant of the LORD your God, which He commanded you,
and go and serve other gods and bow down to them, the
LORD'S anger will burn against you, and you will quickly
perish from the good land He has given you."*[2]

Having entered Canaan, the children of Israel failed in their
task of driving out the tribes already there, finding the project
too difficult. In many cases, they put their defeated enemies
to work as forced labour, but God was not pleased with this
compromise. In Judges they receive this rebuke from the
angel of the Lord: *"I brought you up out of Egypt and led you
into the land I swore to give to your forefathers. I said, 'I will
never break My covenant with you, and you shall not make a
covenant with the people of this land, but you shall break
down their altars.' Yet you have disobeyed Me . . . they will be
thorns in your sides and their gods will be a snare to you."*[3]
In many ways we can see a parallel with a church that is so
often hopelessly compromised, yet puzzled why it is shorn of
power.

Judges is the story of Israel's failures to fully purge the land
of their enemies and of their fascination with the foreign gods
of the region. Time and again, their lifestyles become
polluted and as a result God deserts them, leaving them
subject to foreign rulers. Time and again they cry to God and
He rescues them and they enjoy a period of relative
prosperity.

At one level, the romantic storybook level, this is a book of
daring deeds, a book of heroes: Barak, Gideon, Jepthah and
Samson. They are wonderful stories of fantastic exploits, but
another level of examination tells us a different story. This is
a book of missed opportunities, of failure to follow through,
of civil wars, of quarrels, of people doing just as they please.
I hope you won't think me too jaundiced if I say that it
reminds me of so much recent church history; the rising up
and falling away, the unnecessary quarrels, the failure to carry

2   Joshua 23:11 and 16
3   Judges 2:1-2

things through to completion and the inability to remember God or to acknowledge Him when there have been breakthroughs and victories.

Gideon, for example, for all the wonderful triumph God gave him, made a gold ephod from the earrings captured from the Ishmaelites. He set it up in his home town of Ophrah. The Bible records: *All Israel prostituted themselves by worshipping it there, and it became a snare to Gideon and his family.*[4] He probably thought it was the right thing to do at the time; a means of remembering what God had done for them. But the ephod, not God, soon became the focus. All of us are capable of making similar mistakes—it isn't a question of looking at others and tutting our tongues. In looking at this period in Israel's history, we would do well to remember that.

I wonder whether it's even possible for us to begin to imagine what it was like for this still young nation? How would we have reacted to these peculiar situations? For that matter, how do we react now when choices have to be made? We should not be surprised, when we look at church history, to find times when very little appears to happen. We should not be surprised that much of what has been labelled the charismatic movement has been strong on action and weak on character. Perhaps when we consider these things we will be less hasty in our judgement of the history of Israel.

As we leave the book of Judges, perhaps the most telling epitaph is found in its final verse: *In those days Israel had no king; everyone did as he saw fit.*[5] Does that find a parallel in the Church as we live through the first decade of the 21st century?

Sandwiched between Judges and Samuel, we find the book of Ruth. Its relevance to our study is twofold. Firstly, it shows the grace of God to non-Jews as extended through history; secondly, it shows God's compassion in drawing people of all tribes and nations to Himself. In the story of Rahab the

4 Judges 8:27
5 Judges 21:25

prostitute (Joshua chapters two and six), we already have one example of God's drawing people of other nations to Him; now we find it reflected a second time.

God still judges those who attempt to subvert worship of Him into their own syncretic mix.

As was frequently the case in the region, famine caused families to move. Naomi (a Jewess) travels to Moab with her husband and two sons. Both her sons marry Moabite women after Naomi's husband dies. After a further ten years the husbands both die, and Naomi decides to move back to Judah. She tells her daughters to go back to their own people and tribes, but Ruth the Moabitess replies: *"Where you go I will go, and where you stay I will stay. Your people will be my people and your God my God."*[6]

Realising Ruth is determined on this course of action, Naomi takes her back with her to Israel. Once there, she looks after her mother-in-law, quietly and submissively. While gleaning among the corn she finds herself in the fields of a man named Boaz, a blood relative of Naomi's family. In the tradition of the time, should he wish to marry her, he would be able to do so by purchasing the fields that had passed to Naomi on the death of her husband. This would preserve the family line.

Yet when we read this story, it is apparent this is no dogged pursuit through a misplaced sense of duty to a dead relative and his widow. Boaz's response is of deep human emotion in one of the most touching love stories of the Bible. In fact, his pursuit of her hand is far from certain, as there is another blood relative who has an even closer claim to the land (and therefore to Ruth). It is only when the unnamed relative

6   Ruth 1:16

declines to pursue the offer that Boaz is free to marry her. When he makes his intentions clear before the elders they reply: *"May the LORD make the woman who is coming into your home like Rachel and Leah, who together built up the house of Israel. May you have standing in Ephrathah and be famous in Bethlehem. Through the offspring the LORD gives you by this young woman, may your family be like that of Perez, whom Tamar bore to Judah."* [7]

The truth of this wonderful prophetic chapter is found in the last few verses of the book. *This, then, is the family line of Perez: Perez was the father of Hezron, Hezron the father of Ram, Ram the father of Amminadab, Amminadab the father of Nahshon, Nahshon the father of Salmon, Salmon the father of Boaz, Boaz the father of Obed, Obed the father of Jesse, and Jesse the father of David.* [8] What a wonderful response these simple acts of love and obedience provoke from God. Both Boaz and Ruth (even as a foreigner), find themselves part of the lineage of Jesus Christ. That too, is the inheritance of everyone who follows God in simple love and obedience. Beyond that, this brief tale of life shows that God had not forgotten His promises to the people He still called His own. Despite the erratic nature of their response to Him, He was still working His purposes out.

From Ruth we move on to a colossus of the Bible—Samuel. As we come to the life of Samuel, who was dedicated to God by his mother Hannah, we find Israel once more at a low spiritual and physical ebb. *In those days the Word of the LORD was rare; there were not many visions.* [9]

Eli, a saintly but weak man into whose hands Samuel has been entrusted from an early age, is unable to control his own sons, who have abused their positions as priests. Eli's sons stand in stark contrast to the dedication of Samuel, growing up in the temple courts from infancy, and rapidly recognised as an upright young man with a clear, prophetic gift. God tells

---

7   Ruth 4:11-12
8   Ruth 4:18-22
9   1 Samuel 3:1

Samuel he is going to remove Eli's sons from service.

Finally the day comes when Israel once more faces conflict with the Philistines. The army send for the Ark to go with them into battle, accompanied by Eli's two sons. Eli, by this time an old man, his sight almost gone, sits fearfully by the roadside, waiting for news of the day's events. On hearing that Israel are defeated, the Ark captured and his sons killed, he tumbles from his chair, the fall breaking his neck.

However, the captured Ark brings the Philistines nothing but trouble. Wherever they send it, plague breaks out and so, through God's supernatural intervention, the Ark is returned to Israel. Though we may not see such dramatic demonstrations of God's power today, we do well to remember that God still judges those who attempt to subvert worship of Him into their own syncretic religious mix.

As Samuel judged the people, Israel once again learnt to worship God, but even though Samuel brought some much-needed wisdom and direction to the people on his annual journey throughout Israel, the people began to long for a king, so that they could be like the nations round about them. A coming kingship had already been predicted by Jacob, but at the same time Samuel sees this as rejection of his own role and is hurt by it. God tells Samuel: *"It is not you they have rejected, but they have rejected Me as their king."*[10]

If we pause there a moment, we will see that God is making an astonishing statement—He is their true king. Understanding the significance of that enables us to understand the significance of Jesus, *"The Lion of the tribe of Judah."*[11] However, at this stage in their history, God makes it clear that in demanding their own way the Israelites want to have someone who fits their pre-conception of what a king should be like; someone who is very much like them. We see so much of that in our modern political scene. Ultimately it will be God's kingdom, God's rule and God's authority that

10   1 Samuel 8:7
11   Revelation 5:5

is seen on earth, but meanwhile, man always thinks he knows better than God.

Nonetheless, a king the Israelites have asked for and a king they will have. Again, God's mercy is apparent, as He takes the very thing they have asked for in rebellion and uses it to bring His plan for mankind closer to fruition. The establishment of a royal line will bring us to the next step in the preparation for the coming of the Messiah.

Returning to our story we discover that Saul, a young man from the tribe of Benjamin, is chosen by God to lead Israel. In summarizing his character, it is not my intention to dismiss him or label him in any way that suggests we are superior. The lessons of Saul's life are scriptural. The challenge for us is to allow God to examine our hearts and change us, not for us to feel smug about the failure of a man who started so well.

It is sufficient to say here that Saul is one of the great tragic figures of the Bible. A man physically head and shoulders above all the other men, humble at the outset, in awe of responsibility, he ended his life alienated from God and his fellow men, consulting with a medium on the eve of a battle that cost both his life and the life of his sons. Yet God would have used Saul if he had remained obedient. Samuel told Saul: *"You have not kept the command the LORD your God gave you; if you had, He would have established your kingdom over Israel for all time. But now your kingdom will not endure."*[12]

What a tragedy! What an epitaph—*"Your kingdom will not endure."* What was at the heart of the problem?—Pride and disobedience. Saul wanted to be honoured before men more than he wanted to honour God and acknowledge his sin. He got to the stage where he didn't think he needed to wait for Samuel, God's servant, the prophet who had anointed him. Saul thought he could do it all himself. But Samuel, in speaking with Saul, touched a chord that applies equally to us

12   1 Samuel 13:13-14

all: *"Does the LORD delight in burnt offerings and sacrifices as much as in obeying the voice of the LORD? To obey is better than sacrifice . . ."*[13]

Although our subject is Israel, this tragic story is a challenge that should cause us to stop and ask what motivates us. However involved we are in Christian ministry, are we really trying to please God, or are we more concerned about ourselves and how we appear to others?

Saul's choice reflected the dilemma that continued to face the nation of Israel. The problem of whether Israel would follow God's laws or man's ways was to be a recurring theme for the Jewish nation and the kings who would follow.

13   I Samuel 15:22

Chapter 7

THE DAVIDIC KINGDOM

The LORD is my light and my salvation—whom shall I fear?
The LORD is the stronghold of my life—of whom shall I be
afraid?

Psalm 27:1

Even a cursory study of David shows us how important it is
to fully understand the line of kingship God has ordained, as
it may be totally at odds with our own idea of the ideal king.

Of all the men in the Bible we have met so far, David stands
out as one who is swept hither and thither by events and
circumstances. The paradox is in that in the midst of all this
turmoil, David is a man who keeps his eyes fixed on the Lord.

When Samuel was instructed by God to secretly go to Jesse's
family and there anoint the future king of Israel, Samuel had
no idea God had chosen David. Even as a man of God he
judged Jesse's sons on appearance. He was convinced Eliab
would be the Lord's anointed one, but God told him: *"The*
LORD does not look at the things man looks at. Man looks at
the outward appearance, but the LORD looks at the heart."[1]

Having been secretly anointed, David, a skilled musician,
finds himself called to the court of the king; Saul. By this
time judgement has already been passed on Saul's kingship
and God has begun to withdraw His presence and protection.
Saul is unaware of what has passed between Samuel and
David. David is to minister before King Saul in music, to
soothe Saul when an evil spirit troubles him. For a while,

1   1 Samuel 16:7

David's playing is sufficient to quieten the king, but with the passing of time and Saul's continued spiritual decline, even David's playing appears to have no effect.

As Saul continues his slide into disgrace, David begins to take centre-stage. Confident in God's ability to give victory whatever the seeming odds, David's defeat of Goliath brings him national fame. Although Saul is delighted to be freed from the taunting of the Philistines, and promotes David to a place of prominence in the army, he cannot bear to be outshone by him, and when he is greeted by the women of the towns singing; *"Saul has slain his thousands and David his tens of thousands,"*[2] anger and jealousy take the place of appreciation.

Thwarted in his attempts to kill David by subterfuge, he twice tries to pin him to the wall in the palace by throwing a spear. Jonathan, the king's son and David's closest friend, warns David that his father means to kill him. Despite Saul's employment of thousands of Israel's finest troops, God protects David. These events are, in themselves, a wonderful example of God's saving grace and a demonstration that the pathway to receiving what God has promised is not always smooth.

After Saul's death in battle, David is proclaimed King of Judah then, after further civil war, King of all Israel. Finally, after many years, Samuel's prophetic anointing of David comes to fruition as he governs the kingdom.

At last, after David is *settled in his palace and the LORD had given him rest from all his enemies*[3] God speaks to David through Nathan the prophet, declaring: *"I will make your name great, like the names of the greatest men of the earth . . . 'I will raise up your offspring to succeed you . . . I will establish the throne of his kingdom forever . . . When he does wrong, I will punish him . . . but My love will never be taken from him . . . Your house and your kingdom will endure forever before Me; your throne will be established forever.'"*[4]

---

2   1 Samuel 18:7
3   2 Samuel 7:1
4   2 Samuel 7:9-16 extracted

Here, in this passage, we discover God re-affirming and reinforcing the promises already made to the patriarchs and here we begin to see a fulfilment of Jacob's prophetic words concerning Judah. Let us examine four specific promises of God to David found in this passage:

- David's name will be known throughout the world
- His house (that is, his own descendants) will endure forever
- His throne will be established forever
- His kingdom will be established forever

Three times the 'forever' of God is confirmed in the passage, alongside the promise that God's love will never be removed from David's descendants. Once again God is dealing in the absolutes that the sceptics, in the age we live, find hard to comprehend. We see that God's previously established promises remain unshakeable with the passage of years. Over these promises, God lays further foundations for the coming of the Messiah.

In case you think we have forgotten Israel, and this is in danger of becoming a ramble through the heroes and heroines of the Old Testament, we look now at David's prophetic prayer, given in response to God's promises. In the midst of that prayer, found in 2 Samuel, we find these words: *"And who is like Your people Israel—the one nation on earth that God went out to redeem as a people for Himself . . . You have established Your people as Your very own forever, and You, O LORD, have become their God."*[5] Note the possessive nature of God's relationship with Israel. They are:

- Your people Israel
- A people for Himself (God)
- Your people
- Your very own forever

5   2 Samuel 7:23-24

David, in concluding, affirms: *"O Sovereign LORD, you are God! Your words are trustworthy, and You have promised these good things to Your servant. Now be pleased to bless the house of Your servant, that it may continue forever in Your sight; for You, O Sovereign LORD, have spoken, and with Your blessing the house of Your servant will be blessed forever."*[6] David had absolute certainty in God. We need that same certainty as we read the Word of God today.

Your house and your kingdom shall endure forever before Me; your throne shall be established forever.

Time passes and David, as most of you reading this will know, fails to maintain the standards God has set. Seeing Bathsheba, the wife of another man, bathing on her rooftop, he is smitten by her beauty and sends to have her brought to his palace. She consents to this and sleeps with the king. Discovering she is pregnant, Bathsheba sends David word about the situation. David has Uriah (Bathsheba's husband) brought back from the battlefield. On two occasions he gets Uriah drunk, in the hope that he will go back to his wife and having had sexual intercourse, not notice the disparity in the time to the birth. When this plan fails, he sends Uriah back to the front-line, conducting a devious campaign that results in Uriah's inevitable death. What, you say, can be worse than this? How can God countenance such an act? Surely David deserves to die, according to the law of the day?

We have to remind ourselves of God's words to Samuel— *God looks on the heart.* Yet many will still say—'but God is countenancing murder, adultery and deceit.' Is He? When Nathan reveals David's sin to him, David immediately acknowledges that he has sinned against God.

6   2 Samuel 7:28-29

God does not justify the sin. The child born through this illicit relationship dies, David's kingdom is torn apart by civil war and his son, Absalom, whom he loved dearly, is slain in battle. We may pay a heavy price for wilful disobedience, and the potentially catastrophic events that threaten to overwhelm David show this all too clearly. Yet God, knowing David's character, is faithful to the promise He has made and does not cut him off from the kingdom.

Contrast David's immediate admission of sin with that of Saul, who sought to justify himself before Samuel and the people. God has never been interested in the self-righteous, but he has always been interested in the humble and the penitent, whatever their sin. In the Psalms we read how David cried to the Lord: *Create in me a clean heart, O God, and renew a right spirit within me.*[7] God restores sinners who recognise their sin and David's life is a testament to that total forgiveness.

Despite all the storms of David's life (and there are many), he comes to recognise God's eternal purposes more and more. His last words, as recorded in 2 Samuel state: *"Is not my house right with God? Has He not made with me an everlasting covenant, arranged and secured in every part? Will He not bring to fruition my salvation and grant me my every desire?"*[8] David not only understands God's eternal purposes but has an absolute assurance that God is utterly faithful. He knows that what God has ordained will come to pass.

It's good for us to remember, faced with doubts, the long-term view that God has for our lives. God has promised that his purposes for us are for good, not evil. We need to maintain our confidence in that truth, just as we need to remind ourselves of God's faithfulness to the nation of Israel.

Looking forward to Israel's next king, we return to David's relationship with Bathsheba. The depth of God's forgiveness

7   Psalm 51:10
8   2 Samuel 23:5

and mercy are demonstrated through the next child of the union between David and Bathsheba. We find that it is Solomon, Bathsheba's second son by David, who is chosen to lead Israel on David's death.

Even atheists and agnostics have heard of Solomon's wisdom. When God visited Solomon and told him he might ask him for anything, Solomon, recognising the daunting task of governing the nation of Israel, asked God for wisdom to rule over the people wisely. Once again, the benefit of hindsight enables us to observe that the sensuality and lure of foreign wives (and their many foreign gods) corrupted his wisdom and discernment. There are others who say that he inherited the hard-won success of his father. Both statements have some truth in them, but let's remember that Solomon asked God for wisdom in order to rule over Israel with fairness and justice. I am sure that the woman whose baby was stolen from her in the night, was grateful for Solomon's wisdom. Once more there is a hint of the character of the Messiah, in the servant nature of this fabulously wealthy king.

For ourselves, we should appreciate the king's desire to serve the people and remember that first and foremost when we assess Solomon's legacy. Let's be honest, how often do we really desire spiritual gifts to serve our fellow believers and how often do we want them to dazzle and impress others with our position and importance?

Similarly, there are those who are so puffed-up with the sense of their own importance that they see all the promises of God for Israel as theirs and deny they have anything to do with the nation of Israel, despite God's frequently repeated, permanent covenants. In that light, it is interesting to note how Solomon saw the nations of his day, even without personal experience of the gospel of Jesus Christ.

The first temple, built during Solomon's lifetime, was the most beautiful man-made building the world has ever seen.

After its completion came its dedication to God. Solomon's prayer begins with a declaration of God's unique nature: *"O LORD, God of Israel, there is no God like you in heaven above or on earth below—You who keep Your covenant of love with Your servants who continue wholeheartedly in Your way."*[9] Two aspects of that opening statement should be kept in mind —Israel's need to continue wholeheartedly before God and God's covenant, given out of pure love.

Is not my house right with God? Has He not made with me an everlasting covenant, arranged and secured in every part? Will He not bring to fruition my salvation and grant me my every desire?

As it continues, the prayer becomes an appeal to God for forgiveness in the face of sin—the sin that Solomon, speaking through the Holy Spirit, knows people will commit. He pleads with God:

- When Israel has been defeated by an enemy and they confess their sin—forgive
- When there is no rain because the people have sinned and they confess—forgive
- When famine or plague comes, or an enemy besieges them and they confess their sin—forgive
- When they sin against You and repent and confess— forgive[10]

If Solomon's request to God for wisdom strikes a chord that draws us towards the wisdom of the Messiah, Solomon's plea for mercy finds an immediate echo in the words of Jesus on

---

9   1 Kings 8:23
10   1 Kings Chapter 8

the cross, when he calls out, *"Father, forgive them, for they do not know not what they are doing."*[11]

Solomon's prayer, alongside that of Jesus, is one of the most moving prayers of the Bible, a prayer that spans the ages and speaks of the sins of the nation, but clings to the conviction that for all sin there is a remedy in God's never-ending love. What do we do in our churches about standing in the gap and asking God to forgive?

But remarkable as Solomon's pleas are for Israel, even more arresting is the echo of God's heart for all mankind, expressed in His desire to draw all men to Himself. Solomon continues in prayer: *"As for the foreigner who does not belong to Your people Israel but has come from a distant land because of Your name . . . when he comes and prays towards this temple, then hear from heaven, Your dwelling place, and do whatever the foreigner asks of You, so that all the peoples of the earth may know Your name and fear You, as do Your own people Israel."*[12]

It is remarkable for its inconclusiveness, it is remarkable for its generosity of spirit and it is remarkable as a prophetic foreshadowing of Christ's plea to the disciples to take the gospel into all the earth. As for Israel, once more they are called: *Your own people.* Let's remember that it was presented to God, by the king of Israel, on behalf of the people of Israel. The nation wanted to see the Lord's blessing shared with other nations. That desire to see others blessed by knowing God has eternal significance in the light of that singular nation.

Again though, in dipping into the life of Solomon, we must make sure we present a balanced picture. In the chapter that follows the passage we have just discussed, we read that the Lord once more appears to Solomon. He tells Solomon that as long as Israel walk after God He will be with them, but He issues a solemn warning about failure to continue in this way:

11　Luke 23:34
12　1 Kings 8:41-43

"I will cut off Israel from the land that I have given them and will reject this temple I have consecrated for My Name. Israel will then become a byword and an object of ridicule among all nations. And though this temple is now so imposing, all who pass by will be appalled and will scoff."[13]

We need to see that those warnings, which applied to Israel, apply also to us. We have forgiveness of sins, but if we become indifferent to God and His call on our lives, we cannot expect to maintain His blessing and protection, though He is immensely patient before He brings judgement.

With the death of Solomon, the king's wisdom is soon forgotten. The son chosen as Solomon's heir, in an unwise attempt to show himself strong, ignores the advice of the elder statesmen and as a result fractures the kingdom, with the tribes splitting into the Northern and Southern kingdoms.

The remaining account of Kings and Chronicles is an outline of Israel's spiral into division, destruction, civil war and their eventual conquest and exile. It was a pattern God had warned of, but those following Solomon chose to ignore it. In the division, God separated Judah and Jerusalem from the Northern tribes.

There were at least some kings of Judah who tried to bring the people back to God and who wanted to worship the Lord. The prophets guided many of them. While a particular prophet was alive or gave them advice, they managed to follow God, but their walk was not always consistent. Among the kings who tried to honour God we can think of Asa, Jehosophat, Amaziah, Uzziah, Jotham and, more determinedly, Hezekiah and Josiah. Under these kings God gave Judah victory over their enemies and at certain times they were a very powerful and formidable power in the region. Unfortunately, the kingly line of descent lacked consistency and eventually, in about 590BC (some give the

13   1 Kings 9:7-8

date as 586BC), Jerusalem was captured and many of its leading people taken into exile in Babylon.

It is from the prophets, witnessing and grieving over so many of these events, and not the kings, that we learn God's heart for His people, Israel.

Chapter 8

PROMISE AND HOPE IN THE PROPHETIC PSALMS

My God, my God, why have you forsaken Me? Why are you so far from saving me, so far from the words of my groaning? O My God, I cry out by day, but You do not answer, by night, and am not silent. Yet You are enthroned as the Holy One; You are the praise of Israel.

Psalm 22:1-3

Before moving on to the prophets, we find the theme of the Messiah, and His coming kingdom, running like a thread through the Psalms, with their promises to Israel and to all mankind. Some may be puzzled to sees the Psalms classified as prophetic, yet we should not be surprised that they contain a prophetic seam, for we have already seen that in many passages of the Old Testament God has spoken of the future through those He has filled with the Holy Spirit.

Psalm 2 declares: *The kings of the earth take their stand . . . against the LORD . . . the one enthroned in heaven laughs; the Lord scoffs at them . . . I have installed My King on Zion, My Holy hill . . . He said to Me, "You are My Son; today I have become Your Father. Ask of Me, and I will make the nations Your inheritance, the ends of the earth Your possession. You will rule them with an iron sceptre" . . . Therefore, you kings, be wise . . . serve the LORD with fear . . . Kiss the Son, lest He be angry and you be destroyed in your way . . .*[1]

Jacob, as he gave his prophetic blessing in Genesis, referred

---

1   Psalm 2:2-12 extracted

to the sceptre that was Judah's, the sceptre that would be given to the one to whom it belonged—the Messiah. Here, in Psalm two, we not only see that God is jealous for the kingship of the nation, but He is looking forward through history, some 1,000 years, to the coming of His Son, Jesus. Far from being a temporary kingdom, the kingdom God refers to as belonging to Judah is one that is permanent and one that has Jesus at its centre.

I will declare that your love stands firm forever; that You established Your faithfulness in heaven itself.

From Psalm two we turn to the most famous of all the Messianic Psalms, Psalm twenty-two. Written hundreds of years before Jesus faced false trial and conviction, it details much of what physically took place. It begins with the words Jesus cried from the cross: *My God, My God, why have you forsaken Me?*[2] This suffering Messiah, so dissimilar from the one to whom so many Jews were looking, is *scorned by men and despised by the people . . . they hurl insults, shaking their heads: "He trusts in the LORD, let the LORD rescue Him."*[3] This Messiah is *poured out like water, and all (His) bones are out of joint . . . They have pierced (His) hands and (His) feet . . . They divide (His) garments among them and cast lots for (His) clothing.*[4] This is a Messiah who turns human logic about strength on its head and by a selfless sacrifice draws both Jew and Gentile to Himself. This is Jesus Christ, the Messiah of whom Paul writes in Philippians: *Who, being in very nature God, did not consider equality with God something to be grasped, but made Himself nothing, taking the very nature of a servant, being made in human likeness. And being found in appearance as a man, He humbled Himself and became*

2   Psalm 22:1
3   Psalm 22:6-7
4   Psalm 22:14,16 and 18

obedient to death—even death on a cross! Therefore God exalted Him to the highest place and gave Him the name that is above every name, that at the name of Jesus every knee should bow, in heaven and on earth and under the earth, and every tongue confess that Jesus Christ is Lord, to the glory of God the Father.[5]

What can we say of this Messiah?

- God has installed Him as King
- Kings and nations need to acknowledge Him
- He will be rejected and put to death
- He will be the most humble of men
- God has exalted Him above all things
- Every knee will bow to Him
- He is the Lord Jesus Christ
- He brings glory to the Father

From mere outline, God is now sketching in the details of the unlikely king who is going to shake the very foundations of the spiritual world and bring a message of grace that will transform the future for those who have ears to hear. With the future of the Messiah established at the heart of the nation, let us now consider a few verses (among the many we might have chosen) that express the heart-cry of God for Israel, coursing through the poetic songs that make up the Psalms:

Oh that salvation for Israel would come out of Zion! When the LORD restores the fortunes of His people, let Jacob rejoice and let Israel be glad![6]

The earth is the LORD'S, and everything in it, the world, and all who live in it; for He founded it upon the seas and established it upon the waters.[7]

The LORD foils the plans of the nations; He thwarts the purposes of the peoples. But the plans of the LORD stand firm

---

5   Philippians 2:6-11
6   Psalm 14:7
7   Psalm 24:1-2

forever, the purposes of His heart through all generations. Blessed is the nation whose God is the LORD, the people He chose for His inheritance.[8]

What do these scriptures tell us?

- God will restore the fortunes of His people
- Everything in the earth belongs to the Lord
- God foils the plans of nations
- God's purposes stand for all time
- The people whom God has chosen are blessed by God

Let's pause briefly and consider this rebuttal of nations gathering together in their various groupings. It doesn't matter what forum of nations gather together—the so-called super power of America with its allies, the United Nations, the European Union, the Arab League—God will ultimately thwart the plans of everyone who opposes His purposes. When everything around us seems bleak, we need to remember that God is still on the throne.

Churchill, speaking during the Second World War, when its outcome still didn't seem clear to many people, had this to say; 'It may not be the end, it may not even be the beginning of the end, but it is the end of the beginning.' We need an eternal light to focus our thoughts, not on present situations, but God's future plans.

Not only do the psalmists tell us that God confounds the nations, but Israel are blessed because they are God's possession. We shall see how jealously God guards that relationship as we continue.

I will sing of the LORD's great love forever; with my mouth I will make Your faithfulness known through all generations. I will declare that Your love stands firm forever; that You established Your faithfulness in heaven itself.[9]

8   Psalm 33:10-12
9   Psalm 89:1-2

He remembers His covenant forever, the word He commanded for a thousand generations, the covenant He made with Abraham, the oath He swore to Isaac. He confirmed it to Jacob as a decree, to Israel as an everlasting covenant: "To you I will give the land of Canaan, as the portion you will inherit."[10]

The last Psalm from which we have quoted, Psalm 105, is one of the great legal documents of the Bible. If we have found God emphatic about His promises in the past then this, in summary, is the seal of the documentation.

- Three times we are told it is God's covenant

- We are told it is a covenant forever

- We are told it is an everlasting covenant

- We are told God has commanded it

- We are told God has sworn an oath on it

- We are told God has confirmed it as a decree

- We are told it is for eternity, or as the language here more poetically puts it—a thousand generations

- We are told it is the portion Israel will inherit

For those who would argue that a thousand generations does not equate to eternity, the very least period of time that it could be biblically would be twenty-five thousand years from the time of its inception, some three thousand years ago! What is the central crux of this legally binding document? None other than the land of Canaan, *'the portion Israel will inherit.'*

I am at a loss as to how some theologians try to explain away such scripture. We might have taken other examples from the Psalms, where God speaks of His faithfulness and righteousness, His care for his people, Israel, but this Psalm is so clear as to be incapable of misinterpretation, unless we are

10   Psalm 105:8-11

deliberately looking to ignore the truth. Canaan belongs to Israel forever. God has promised it and God will keep His Word, even if it means disappointing the nations of the world.

As we come towards the close of this very brief glance at the Psalms, we find Psalm 136, dealing with God's plans and protection of Israel. Twenty-six times we find the expression *'His love endures forever.'* It is as if a rather uncertain bride asks her husband again and again if he really loves her, in order to hear the assurance of the words, 'You know I do!' Here, to the doubts of the nation, God responds as that lover, declaring His everlasting love for His people, Israel.

We finish with four more scriptures from the latter stages of the Psalms:

'Pray for the peace of Jerusalem: "May those who love you be secure."' [11]

'As the mountains surround Jerusalem, so the Lord surrounds his people both now and for evermore.' [12]

'For the Lord has chosen Jacob to be His own, Israel to be His treasured possession.' [13]

'He has revealed His Word to Jacob, His laws and decrees to Israel. He has done this for no other nation . . .' [14]

God is once more illustrating the uniqueness of Israel and the Jewish people.

To claim, as some are keen to do, that the promises we have read refer to the church and not to Israel, is to do such violence to the text as to make any understanding of scripture a matter of personal interpretation rather than clear, simple truth. Just because we have heard doctrine preached from a pulpit, does not mean it has a foundation in scripture. We need to make sure we study the whole Word of God to see whether what we have been told is true, rather than existing

11   Psalm 122:6
12   Psalm 125:2
13   Psalm 135:4
14   Psalm 147:19-20

on a diet of second-hand teaching. It is to some of these neglected canons of the Bible that we now turn.

Chapter 9

ISAIAH: GOD'S JUDGEMENTS, GOD'S REDEMPTION

Yet, O LORD, You are our Father. We are the clay, You are the potter; we are all the work of Your hand. Do not be angry beyond measure, O LORD; do not remember our sins forever. Oh, look upon us, we pray, for we are all Your people.

Isaiah 64:8-9

We come now to what is considered the greatest prophetic book of the Bible, that of the prophet Isaiah. He spoke to Judah and Israel for some sixty years, from about 740 to 680 BC. While God used him to speak to both parts of the divided kingdom, his primary focus and commission was to the people of Judah and Jerusalem.

In his lifetime he saw the overthrow of the Northern kingdom of Israel and I am sure it must have been a source of deep grief and real sorrow. The prophets of old, contrary to what some would have us believe, did not take great delight in foretelling disaster. Above everything, they wanted their fellow countrymen to hear what God was saying and they wanted them to do something about it. We too can hear the Word of God and, failing to act upon it, all too easily find ourselves repeating history.

The sixty-six chapters that make up the book of Isaiah may be divided (in very general terms) into two sections:

- Rebellion—warnings—judgement
- Repentance—forgiveness—hope

The first thirty-nine chapters deal in those same general terms with judgement. The last twenty-seven, beginning as they do with that plea of comfort for God's people, ring out with forgiveness, hope, God's eternal kingdom and the coming of the Messiah. Although the Bible wasn't written in chapters, it's a fascinating little by-line that the first thirty-nine chapters are equivalent to the number of books in the Old Testament and the last twenty-seven to the number of books in the New Testament, mirroring both God's old and new covenants.

Isaiah wastes no time on the niceties of introduction. From the outset the language is an unequivocal challenge about the state of the nation. Isaiah begins by referring to Israel as 'a people who do not understand' . . . *(a) sinful nation, a people loaded with guilt* . . . (a people with) *no soundness.*[1] The prophet warns the people that God is tired of their festivals and sacrifices: *I cannot bear your evil assemblies . . . your appointed feasts my soul hates . . . I am weary of bearing them.*[2] He tells them their *hands are full of blood.*[3] God, through His prophet Isaiah, urges them to change their hearts, before God's judgements fall on them. What a description of the heart of the nation.

- Without understanding
- With no soundness
- Laden with guilt
- Religiously bankrupt
- Guilty of shedding innocent blood

I can't help but wonder how close some of our nations are to that very same description.

Yet, even in the midst of this crushing indictment, God reveals His plans for their future. *In the last days the*

---

1   Isaiah 1:3,4 and 6 extracted
2   Isaiah 1:13-14 extracted
3   Isaiah 1:15

mountain of the LORD'S Temple will be established as chief among the mountains: it will be raised above the hills, and all nations will stream to it. Many peoples will come and say, "Come, let us go up to the mountain of the LORD, to the House of the God of Jacob. He will teach us His ways, so that we may walk in His paths." The law will go out from Zion, the Word of the LORD from Jerusalem.[4]

There is hope for the future:

- In the last days the Lord's Temple will be established
- All nations will stream to it
- It will be known as the Mountain of the Lord
- It will be called the House of the God of Jacob
- The Messiah will teach men His ways
- The Word of the Lord will go out from Jerusalem

God's plan for the *last days* places Jerusalem at its very centre. It is referred to as the house of the God of Jacob, the title given whenever reference is made to the lineage and inheritance of the twelve tribes. Again, we need to remember these prophetic promises as we see God's judgement fall on His people. The question we have to ask ourselves is whether the judgement is final and overrides the promise, or whether the judgement is for a time (a purifying agent), until God restores His people?

In chapter nine, in the midst of further dire warnings of judgement, we come across that wonderful passage of scripture, so often read in our churches, but rarely fully grasped in meaning: *The people walking in darkness have seen a great light; on those living in the land of the shadow of death a light has dawned.*[5] Once more we find God's great inclusive promise to the Gentiles, foretold in this verse that hints at the coming of the Messiah. The passage continues: *For to us a Child is born, to us a Son is given, and the government will be on His shoulders. And He will be called Wonderful Counsellor, Mighty God, Everlasting Father,*

4   Isaiah 2:2-3
5   Isaiah 9:2

*Prince of Peace. Of the increase of His government and peace
there shall be no end. He will reign on David's throne and
over His kingdom, establishing it and upholding it with
justice and righteousness from that time on and forever. The
zeal of the LORD Almighty will accomplish this.*[6]

One is in awe of the titles that God gives to His Son, Jesus
Christ, in this passage. Their four strands emphasise the
completeness of both kingly and priestly authority:

- Jesus is wonderful counsellor and Prince of Peace
- The breaker down of the middle wall of partition
- The intercessor for all who believe in him
- Authority to rule is His and His alone

And there is more. Jesus is to reign on David's throne as a
descendant of David, as we have already seen promised. He
is to rule over David's kingdom, the kingdom promised to the
patriarchs, the land of Canaan.

Isaiah chapter ten warns that only a remnant will return to the
land after God has punished them. God's punishments are
certain, but His promises are secure for all time. Chapter eleven,
again looking prophetically forward to the Messiah, tells us: *A
shoot will come up from the stump of Jesse; from His roots a
Branch will bear fruit. The Spirit of the LORD will rest upon Him
—the Spirit of wisdom and of understanding, the Spirit of
counsel and of power, the spirit of knowledge and of the fear of
the LORD—and He will delight in the fear of the LORD.*[7] The day
is surely coming, Isaiah continues, when *the earth will be full of
the knowledge of the LORD as the waters cover the sea.*[8]

Not only that, but this root of Jesse will stand as a *banner for
the peoples; . . . In that day the Lord will reach out His hand
a second time to reclaim the remnant that is left of His
people from Assyria . . . Egypt . . . Babylonia . . . and from the
islands of the sea.'*[9] Before proceeding further in this chapter,
let's consider four distinct aspects of verses ten and eleven:

6   Isaiah 9:6-7
7   Isaiah 11:1-3
8   Isaiah 11:9
9   Isaiah 11:10-11

- Firstly, we should note that it is the root of Jesse that stands as a banner to the peoples. This explicitly shows us the lineage and genealogy of Christ.

- Secondly, it is God who reaches out; the re-gathering of Israel is a sovereign act of God, not dependent upon man's approval, or even man's support.

- Thirdly, the Bible states that this is a second re-gathering. One comment regularly made of Israel is that all her promises are in the past—her return was from Babylon and that took place. There are no prophecies that deal with a future return. This passage points out the absurdity of that claim. Not only is there a second re-gathering but, we are forced to ask, when does it take place in history?

- Fourthly, Israel's second re-gathering is a sign to the Gentile nations.

Even in the light of such scripture, there are those who maintain that the second ingathering took place in the Old Testament. It's a view as full of holes as an old leaky ship, but we can scuttle the craft even more rapidly by looking at our texts from Isaiah eleven. The time of the second ingathering is after the root of Jesse has been revealed; that is, after Jesus has been born. We may argue about the exact ingathering, but we cannot dispute the timescale in which it happens.

In case those reading are still unsure, Isaiah makes God's intentions even plainer in the verses that follow: *He will raise a banner for the nations and gather the exiles of Israel; He will assemble the scattered people of Judah from the four quarters of the earth. Ephraim's jealousy will vanish, and Judah's enemies will be cut off; Ephraim will not be jealous of Judah, nor Judah hostile toward Ephraim.*[10]

The theme of Israel's ultimate salvation continues in the following chapter: *In that day you will say, "I will praise you, O*

LORD. *Although You were angry with me, Your anger has turned away . . . Surely God is my salvation . . . Sing to the LORD, for He has done glorious things; let this be known to all the world. Shout aloud and sing for joy, people of Zion, for great is the Holy One of Israel among you."*[11] Nor is this theme completed yet. Moving on two chapters we read: *The Lord will have compassion on Jacob; once again He will choose Israel and will settle them in their own land. Aliens will join them and unite with the House of Jacob. . . And the House of Israel will possess the nations.*[12] All of this is hardly the language we would associate with final rejection. In summary, these scriptures tell us:

- God's anger will turn away from Israel
- God will have compassion on His people
- God will gather the exiles of Israel
- They will come from all over the globe
- He will settle them in the land of Canaan
- People from other nations will join them

As we glance through these opening chapters of Isaiah, dealing as they do with the judgement and punishment of Israel, we see how even here veins of grace and mercy are still flowing from God to His people.

We discover too, that God's judgements are not confined to Israel. There is much said about the ultimate fate of the kings and nations that surrounded Israel at that time; Babylon, Assyria, Moab, Damascus, Cush, Egypt, Edom and Arabia. The self-same people who often deny that Israel has a future commonly believe that Israel deserves continued punishment. But they become far less certain about the matter when it comes to the Lord's judgement of other nations and other governments. They would do well to remember that God does not judge in isolation.

God's justice and God's day of judgement are fearful. Looking beyond the events of Isaiah's own time, Isaiah gives us glimpses

11   Isaiah 12:1-6 extracted
12   Isaiah 14:1-2

of what that final judgement will be like. *The floodgates of the heavens are opened, the foundations of the earth shake. The earth is broken up, the earth is split asunder, the earth is thoroughly shaken . . . it falls—never to rise again. In that day the LORD will punish the powers in the heaven above and the kings on the earth below . . . The moon will be abashed, the sun ashamed; for the LORD Almighty will reign on Mount Zion and in Jerusalem, and before its elders, gloriously.*[13]

Once more we see Jerusalem as the centre and the Lord Himself reigning. After judgement will come restoration. As we carry on reading through Isaiah we begin to see a pattern emerging in these chapters: inevitable judgement but final deliverance for future generations. This time the people will not be driven out: *In days to come Jacob will take root, Israel will bud and blossom and fill all the world with fruit.*[14]

That theme is repeated two chapters later: *Therefore this is what the LORD, who redeemed Abraham, says to the House of Jacob: "No longer will Jacob be ashamed; no longer will their faces grow pale. When they see among them their children, the work of My hands, they will keep My name holy; they will acknowledge the holiness of the Holy One of Jacob, and will stand in awe of the God of Israel."*[15]

Again and again it is God who is the initiator: He promises redemption; He declares what He will do in times to come – it is God who commits Himself to covenant.

But future prosperity does not excuse them from God's voice of judgement railing against their present sin. Isaiah returns

13   Isaiah 24:18-23
14   Isaiah 27:6
15   Isaiah 29:22-23

to the language of the opening verses of the book. Their contempt for God and His laws is like a bulging high wall, which will *break in pieces like pottery.*[16] Verse after verse warn about the consequences of continued sin and neglect of God, before surprising us with a marvellous chapter of hope, nestling in the first section of Isaiah.

The desert and the parched land will be glad; the wilderness will rejoice and blossom . . . Water will gush forth in the wilderness and streams in the desert . . . And a highway will be there; it will be called the way of Holiness . . . it will be for those who walk in that Way . . . the redeemed will walk there, and the ransomed of the Lord will return. They will enter Zion with singing; everlasting joy will crown their heads. Gladness and joy will overtake them, and sorrow and sighing

---

There is no one who knows more intimately or who has felt more deeply the suffering of the Jewish people than God Himself.

---

will flee away.[17] Suddenly once more there is hope.

Now I happen to believe that we can have a partial fulfilment of prophecy and then a more complete fulfilment at a later date. You don't have to agree with me and it certainly doesn't undermine the scriptural truth of God's Word. I believe this chapter is just one such passage, just as Old Testament characters (such as Moses) may show us a type of character more fully and perfectly revealed in the Messiah. If we return to this chapter there is no doubt that since the modern state of Israel was recognised in 1948, the desert has indeed blossomed. God's final outworking of this will, I am sure, be far more

16   Isaiah 30:14
17   Isaiah 35,1,6,8,9 and 10 extracted

spectacular, but the first signs are already there for us to see.

There is a further picture hidden in the canvas of this chapter. The prophet Hosea speaks of how God will lead His people into the desert and of how He will allure them, causing them to want to find Him. There is no suggestion they know the purpose of the wilderness experience, but through it God reveals His mercy to them. Is God doing that among His people at this time? What we now see as a trickle of Jews turning to Christ, may well become a gushing stream.

We now turn to consider what I have termed the latter section of Isaiah, whose underlying themes we outlined as repentance, forgiveness and hope. Its tone is set with the opening verses of Isaiah forty: *Comfort ye, comfort ye My people, saith your God. Speak ye comfortably to Jerusalem, and cry unto her, that her warfare is accomplished, that her iniquity is pardoned: for she hath received of the Lord's hand double for all her sins.*[18] Before we continue with the passage, let's consider what is involved in this statement.

- Firstly, there is the imperative command, twice repeated—Comfort ye, comfort ye

- Secondly we are told how we are to comfort her—We are to let her know her warfare is accomplished and her iniquity (sin) pardoned

- That only leaves us with God's part in all this: *she hath received of the Lord's hand double for all her sins.'*

It was a common tradition at this time that when a man was in debt, a list would be nailed to a post or to his possessions, stating the claim others had against him. If a richer relative wished to redeem that pledge, he was able to fold the skin or parchment over and nail it together, signifying that he covered those debts. What a wonderful picture of God's putting away the charges against Israel.

18   Isaiah 40:1-2 (King James)

Comfort ye, comfort ye My people, saith your God. Speak ye comfortably to Jerusalem, and cry unto her, that her warfare is accomplished, that her iniquity is pardoned: for she hath received of the Lord's hand double for all her sins.

But let's return to these words. There are only two logical conclusions we can draw from this extraordinary passage: Isaiah was either seriously wrong about hearing God, or God had a message He wanted all mankind to hear. If it is the first then we are all in trouble! If it is, as I believe, the second, then who do you suppose should be doing the comforting? I believe it should be the church. We have been entrusted as guardians of God's Word to make sure people hear the gospel clearly. Now, as we near the end of the age, we need to ensure that Israel hears that heart-cry from God. Nor does God intend this as some hole-in-the-wall operation. Verse nine of the same chapter exhorts: *You who bring good tidings to Zion, go up on a high mountain. You who bring good tidings to Jerusalem, lift up your voice with a shout . . . say to the towns of Judah, "Here is your God!"*[19]

What is God's involvement in all this? We find our answer in the following chapter, where God addresses His people in these words: *"Do not be afraid, O worm Jacob, O little Israel, for I Myself will help you," declares the LORD, your Redeemer, the Holy One of Israel.*[20] God is actively involved in this agenda.

If those verses from chapters forty and forty-one are a source of comfort, chapter forty-three is a reinforcement of those

19   Isaiah 40:9
20   Isaiah 41:14

themes. Little commentary is needed, so transparently does God reveal His heart towards Israel. *But now this is what the Lord says—He who created you, O Jacob, He who formed you, O Israel: "Fear not, for I have redeemed you; I have summoned you by name; you are Mine. When you pass through the waters, I will be with you . . . For I am the Lord, your God, the Holy One of Israel, your Saviour . . . I will give men in exchange for you, and people in exchange for your life. Do not be afraid, for I am with you; I will bring your children from the east and gather you from the west. I will say to the north, 'Give them up!' and to the south, 'Do not hold them back.' Bring My sons from afar and My daughters from the ends of the earth— everyone who is called by My name, whom I created for My glory, whom I formed and made . . . I have revealed and saved and proclaimed . . . I am God"* [21]

Again and again it is God who is the initiator: He promises redemption; He declares what He will do in times to come— it is God who commits Himself to covenant.

So that there is no doubt, the Lord continues His great redemptive theme. Through Isaiah, he tells His people: *"I am the Lord, your Holy One, Israel's Creator, your King."* [22] Here is yet another example of the multi-faceted aspect of God's declaration:

- He is Israel's Lord
- The Holy One
- Israel's Creator
- Israel's King.

In this continuing heart-cry for His people, God's grief for Israel's sin recognises their own inability to save themselves. In this matter too, it is God who will act: *"I, even I, am He who blots out your transgressions, for My own sake, and remembers your sins no more."* [23]

---

21 Isaiah 43:1-12 extracted
22 Isaiah 43:15
23 Isaiah 43:25

When people are led to look at Israel, they often don't like what they see, or don't like what they read about their history. On the basis of their own understanding they decide that God won't be interested in the nation anymore. Such people miss the point. God is jealous for His name. God has committed Himself and whatever man might think, God will stand on those promises for His own name's sake.

That does not mean that we wear rose-tinted glasses and pretend God never intended to deal with Israel. That would ignore all we have read in the opening chapters of Isaiah. Nor can we paint a picture of superficial restoration. Even here, in these latter chapters, God is not finished with judgement. In the same chapter from which we have just quoted, we read: *"I will disgrace the dignitaries of your temple, and I will consign Jacob to destruction and Israel to scorn."*[24] Oh yes, judgement was coming, with an inescapable certainty, but it was judgement, not extinction—not total rejection. Here is God, hating the sin and forced to deal with it, but still honouring the covenant, still moved by compassion.

God cannot let the theme alone as His heart is roused. Having rebuked them, He immediately continues with these words: *"But now listen, O Jacob, My servant, Israel, whom I have chosen. This is what the LORD says—He who made you, who formed you in the womb, and who will help you: Do not be afraid, O Jacob, My servant, Jeshurun, whom I have chosen. For I will pour water on the thirsty land, and streams on the dry ground; I will pour out My Spirit on your offspring, and My blessing on your descendants. They will spring up like grass in a meadow, like poplar trees by flowing streams. One will say, 'I belong to the LORD'; another will call himself by the name of Jacob; still another will write on his hand, 'The LORD's', and will take the name Israel. This is what the LORD says—Israel's King and Redeemer, the LORD Almighty: I am the first and the last, apart from Me there is no God."*[25]

---

24   Isaiah 43:28
25   Isaiah 44:1-6

Those verses, quoted in their entirety, summarize God's view of the nation:

- Israel is God's chosen servant
- God formed them
- God will help them
- God will pour His Holy Spirit upon them
- The Lord is Israel's King and Redeemer

God has formed the nation from birth. He has chosen them. He is their King and Redeemer; their Messiah. Their blessing is not limited to the physical; they will receive the Holy Spirit. And then we come upon those marvellous, striking words that we also read in Revelation—*"I am the Alpha and the Omega."*[26] God declares the eternal aspect of His nature in His dealings with His people Israel.

If Isaiah forty-four is breath-taking in its emphasis, what can we say of God's declaration to Cyrus (a non-Jew) in the following chapter? *"For the sake of Jacob My servant . . . I summon you by name and bestow on you a title of honour, though you do not acknowledge Me."*[27] Let's pause for a moment before we continue. What an astonishing statement—I summon you; I bestow on you a title of honour even though you do not acknowledge Me. Oh come on, I hear some cynics say, this is becoming absurd! But wait; do you not recognise the echo of the New Testament?

The Epistle to the Ephesians, speaking of Gentile believers, says this: *As for you, you were dead in your transgressions and sins . . . But because of His great love for us, God, who is rich in mercy, made us alive with Christ even when we were dead in transgressions—it is by grace you have been saved. And God raised us up with Christ and seated us with Him in heavenly realms in Christ Jesus, in order that in the coming ages He might show the incomparable riches of His grace, expressed in his kindness to us in Christ Jesus.*[28] Suddenly it's

26   Revelation 1:8
27   Isaiah 45:4
28   Ephesians 2:1 and 4-7

different. 'Hang on,' I hear people say, 'that is not the same, that is our inheritance in Christ as Gentile believers. Ephesians is written for us.'

Open your eyes! We need to see that the God of the Old Testament, the *'I am that I am; the First and Last,'* is the God of the New Testament, again declared as *I am* and *the First and the Last.* The two do not hang in tension, but in harmony. The grace of the Old Testament, caused in God calling men to Himself, is the grace of the New Testament, equally undeserved and not based on any merit in ourselves.

I believe we often have problems with the Old Testament because we lose sight of the promise of the New. We begin in grace but we end in law. We cannot enter heaven through our own works—no more could Israel. We need to make sure that by our attitude we are not standing in opposition to the plans of God. Isaiah contains a severe warning to those who place themselves in this position: *"Remember this, fix it in mind, take it to heart, you rebels. Remember the former things, those of long ago; I am God, there is no other; I am God, and there is none like Me. I make known the end from the beginning, from ancient times, what is still to come. I say: My purpose will stand, and I will do all that I please."*[29]

One of the problems of a scientific age is that we attempt to reduce everything to our own humanity. We look at the current empirical evidence (what is around us) and we use that as the foundation for our conclusions. Philosophically too, we are caught up in the spirit of the age. To believe in absolutes nowadays, particularly in terms of Christianity, is to run the risk of being called a bigot. We are massively influenced by what we see, hear and read. Most of man's justice and sense of what is right is based in humanism, which stands opposed to the justice and declared order ordained by God. No wonder we have problems with eternal concepts and the unchanging nature of God. God says: *I will grant*

---

29   Isaiah 46:8-10

salvation to Zion, My splendour to Israel.[30] What do you say?

The weight of evidence for God's divine intervention in Israel's affairs grows chapter by chapter through this moving book, as in this example from chapter forty-nine: *But Zion said, "The* Lord *has forsaken me, the Lord has forgotten me." "Can a mother forget the baby at her breast and have no compassion on the child she has borne? Though she may forget, I will not forget you! See, I have engraved you on the palms of My hands; your walls are ever before Me. Your sons hasten back, and those who laid you waste depart from you. Lift up your eyes and look around; all your sons gather and come to you. As surely as I live," declares the* Lord, *"You will wear them all as ornaments; you will put them on, like a bride. Though you were ruined and made desolate and your land laid waste, now you will be too small for your people, and those who devoured you will be far away . . . I will beckon to the Gentiles, I will lift up My banner to the peoples; they will bring your sons in their arms and carry your daughters on their shoulders. . . Then all mankind will know that I, the* Lord, *am your Saviour, your Redeemer, the Mighty One of Jacob."*[31]

The theme continues in subsequent chapters. In chapter fifty-one we hear the Lord thundering in command: *"Listen to me, you who pursue righteousness and who seek the* Lord: *look to the rock from which you were cut . . . look to Abraham . . . The* Lord *will surely comfort Zion and will look with compassion on all her ruins; He will make her deserts like Eden . . . Joy and gladness will be found in her; thanksgiving and the sound of singing."*[32] As Christians, who have come to the Messiah, Jesus, these scriptures are for us. They should instil understanding and provoke a response. Our close involvement is reinforced in the following chapter.

Awake, awake, O Zion, clothe yourself with strength. Put on your garments of splendour, O Jerusalem, the holy city . . . "You were sold for nothing and without money you will be

30   Isaiah 46:13
31   Isaiah 49:14-19,22 and 26
32   Isaiah 51:1-3

redeemed" . . . *How beautiful on the mountains are the feet of*
those who bring good news, who proclaim peace, who bring
good tidings, who proclaim salvation, who say to Zion, "Your
God reigns!"[33] In other words, the prophet is saying, if you
want to align yourself with the purposes of God, you need to
ask what your part is in the outworking of these scriptures.
There are those who would say, "but the facts contradict the
prayer, Israel is not free." It is a legitimate comment, but we
have to move beyond the physical, to the spiritual, in order to
see the physical changed. Daniel was a man in exile, but
when he understood God's purposes he prayed, despite the
evidence of his own eyes. He believed God would do what He
had promised. That sort of perseverance is still one of our
greatest challenges.

We arrive now at one of the greatest prophetic chapters about
the Messiah, the Man who would be the hope of Israel and the
hope for all the Gentiles. With Psalm twenty-two it ranks as one
of the clearest expositions of what awaited Jesus. It was written
some 700 years before His birth. In this chapter we see that the
salvation of Israel is intimately tied up with the salvation of all
mankind. This King of the Jews was to be *despised and*
rejected by men, a man of sorrows, and familiar with
suffering . . . He was to be *oppressed and afflicted.*[34] When we
read this account of Jesus we cannot help but see how closely it
is tied up with the history of God's people over the last two
thousand years—despised, rejected, hounded from land to land,
the victims of hatred and murder.

I am not in any way suggesting that earns them the right to
salvation or that they have any power of salvation: that is in
Jesus Christ alone. What we do see is that their King, their
Messiah, the King of the Jews, has understood and known
their suffering down through the centuries. There is no one
who knows more intimately or who has felt more deeply the
suffering of the Jewish people than God. From this deeply

33   Isaiah 52:1,3 and 7
34   Isaiah 53:3 and 7 extracted

moving chapter, a witness to all humanity of the truth of God's Word and of His love, we return to the theme of God's promises.

---

*How beautiful on the mountains are
the feet of those who bring good
news, who proclaim peace, who bring
good tidings, who proclaim salvation,
who say to Zion,
"Your God reigns!"*

"Enlarge the place of your tent . . . You will spread out to the right and to the left; your descendants will dispossess nations . . . For a brief moment I abandoned you, but with deep compassion I will bring you back . . . with everlasting kindness I will have compassion on you," says the LORD your Redeemer . . . Though the mountains be shaken and the hills be removed, yet My unfailing love for you will not be shaken, nor My covenant of peace be removed," says the LORD, who has compassion on you.[35]

Look at how God declares His heart for His people Israel:

- With deep compassion I will bring you back
- With everlasting love I will have compassion on you
- My unfailing love for you will not be shaken
- My covenant of peace will not be removed

God declares yet again that it is impossible for him to change His mind concerning His promises. Once more we see that His mercy is always available to those who seek Him.

In chapter fifty-nine Isaiah returns to the theme of Israel's Messiah: *"The Redeemer will come to Zion, to those in Jacob*

---

35   Isaiah 54:2,3,7,8 and 10 extracted

who repent of their sins," declares the LORD. *"As for Me, this is My covenant with them," says the* LORD. *"My Spirit, who is on you, and My words that I have put in your mouth will not depart from your mouth, or from the mouths of your children, or from the mouths of their descendants from this time on and forever," says the* LORD.[36] The reality of that scripture is found in our reading it, more than 2,500 years later.

God's promise, made to Isaiah, is a promise we can still accept and claim by faith. God has always reserved to Himself a remnant of His people. Elijah was convinced he was alone, but God told him there were 7,000 others who had not indulged in Baal worship. These verses include an important stipulation—it is to those who repent that God will make himself known. There are no exceptions. Israel will be saved, but their final turning to God has to be in repentance, not in self-righteousness. Isaiah does not make it clear when exactly God will do this, but having reiterated God's promises in the following chapter, the prophet finishes it with these words: *"In its time I will do this swiftly."*[37] So we can be certain that when God acts for His people it will be decisive and rapid.

Chapter sixty-one begins with the words Jesus used as He began His ministry: *The Spirit of the Sovereign* LORD *is on Me, because the* LORD *has anointed Me to preach good news to the poor, He has sent Me to bind up the broken-hearted, to proclaim freedom for the captives and release from darkness for the prisoners, to proclaim the year of the* LORD'S *favour (and the day of vengeance of our God), to comfort all who mourn, and provide for those who grieve in Zion—to bestow on them a crown of beauty instead of ashes, the oil of gladness instead of mourning, and a garment of praise instead of a spirit of despair. They will be called oaks of righteousness, a planting of the* LORD, *for the display of His splendour.*[38] It is surely no accident that when Jesus

---

36   Isaiah 59:20-21
37   Isaiah 60:22
38   Isaiah 61:1-3

announced Himself to the Jewish nation, he did so with the opening words of this chapter, finishing with the declaration that He brought the *'year of the Lord's favour.'*
What is promised to God's people?

- Good news for the poor
- Binding up of the broken-hearted
- Freedom for captives
- Release from darkness for prisoners
- The year of the Lord's favour
- Beauty for ashes
- A garment of praise instead of a spirit of despair

God's plans stand firm throughout the ages. *For Zion's sake I will not keep silent, For Jerusalem's sake I will not remain quiet, till her righteousness shines out like the dawn, . . . you will be called by a new name . . . You will be a crown of splendour in the LORD's hand . . . No longer will they call you Deserted, or name your land Desolate. But you will be called Hephzibah (*I delight in her*) and your land Beulah (*married*); for the Lord will take delight in you . . .*[39]

"Can a country be born in a day or a nation be brought forth in a moment? Yet no sooner is Zion in labour than she gives birth to her children . . . Rejoice with Jerusalem and be glad for her, all you who love her . . . As a mother comforts her child, so will I comfort you; and you will be comforted over Jerusalem" . . . And they will bring all your brothers, from all the nations, to My Holy mountain in Jerusalem as an offering to the Lord . . ."[40]

- God will not keep quiet over Zion
- God will not be silent over Jerusalem
- They will have a new name
- They will be a crown of splendour
- God will delight in the land

---

39   Isaiah 62:1-4 extracted
40   Isaiah 66:8,10,13 and 20 extracted

- God will bring the nation to birth in a day
- Those who love Jerusalem will rejoice over her
- God will comfort his people over Jerusalem
- All the Jewish people will be brought back to the land

So, as we come to the end of Isaiah, we are faced with declaration after declaration of the Lord towards His people; of grace poured out, mercy extended and righteousness restored. We are silenced before the Word of God, amazed and in awe of what He will do as this age draws to an end. There are many, many other passages we could have examined, but in these final verses we see God's intentions summarised. God will judge the earth and its inhabitants; our nations among them, but in the midst of judgement God will remember His promises to His people and will restore Israel.

Many people still alive, witnessed or read about the birth of Israel on that historic day in May, 1948, when the founding fathers of modern day Israel, after the decisive vote of the United Nations, broadcast the declaration of the new state, even as they were about to be plunged into war with their Arab neighbours. We see the return of many Jews (and sometimes whole communities) from distant nations to the land of Israel. Much prophecy still has to be fulfilled, but it is certain that God will do it.

Chapter 10

JEREMIAH: MORE JUDGEMENT, MORE MERCY

The LORD appeared to us in the past, saying: "I have loved you with an everlasting love; I have drawn you with loving-kindness."

Jeremiah 31:3

Like Isaiah, Jeremiah brings us the uncomfortable message of God's judgement on his people, this time specifically on Judah. The opening chapters deal with the coming banishment of the people and the destruction that will sweep through Judah and overwhelm Jerusalem because of the sin of the people. Yet even in God's retribution we find, as we have found elsewhere, the promise of God's eventual salvation for his people. *" . . . I am your husband. I will choose you—one from a town and two from a clan—and bring you to Zion . . . At that time they will call Jerusalem The Throne of the LORD, and all nations will gather in Jerusalem to honour the name of the LORD . . . the house of Judah will join the house of Israel."*[1] This though, is only a minor part of these opening chapters.

We are faced with an undeniable message of judgement and punishment. Why? God's answer is simple. *"It is because they have forsaken My law, which I set before them; they have not obeyed Me or followed My law . . . I will scatter them*

---

1   Jeremiah 3:14-17 extracted

*among nations . . . and I will pursue them with the sword until
I have destroyed them.*"[2] God's warning to Israel has pursued
them through the ages. The sword destroyed everyone in that
generation who thought they were safe if they relied in their
own strength. Those of future generations have been scattered
through the nations. We have only to examine the history of
Europe over the last 1,000 years to see how that has taken
place.

On and on pour Jeremiah's warnings: *The Lord called you a
thriving olive tree with fruit beautiful in form. But with the
roar of a mighty storm He will set it on fire and its branches
will be broken . . . I will forsake My house, abandon My
inheritance; I will give the one I love into the hands of her
enemies.*[3]

Uncomfortably for those nations, they find themselves the
object of God's ultimate vengeance for their part in
destroying Israel's cities and scattering her people. The
nations that want to see Israel destroyed are signing away
their own future. God sees these countries and their peoples
as *senseless and without knowledge,* in contrast to the tribes
of Israel: *He who is the portion of Jacob is not like these, for
He is the maker of all things, including Israel, the tribe of His
inheritance—the LORD Almighty is His name.*[4]

- God makes Himself personally involved
- God is the portion of Jacob
- Israel the tribe of His inheritance

Even when judging the nation, God does not distance Himself
from that personal relationship, much as in the same way
parents don't distance themselves from their children, even
when they have to discipline them. It is Israel's sin God is
punishing, but their rights, as passed on through the
patriarchs, are irrevocable.

As Jeremiah understands something of the ultimate fate of the

2   Jeremiah 9:13-16 extracted
3   Jeremiah 11:16 and 12:7
4   Jeremiah 10:14-16

countries wanting to attack Israel, he is moved to call out to God, *Pour out your wrath on the nations that do not acknowledge You, on the peoples who do not call on Your name.* Why, you may ask, does Jeremiah do this? The answer is given in the following sentence: *For they have devoured Jacob; they have devoured him completely and destroyed his homeland.*"[5] Jeremiah, speaking by the Holy Spirit, was inspired to utter these words. If God does not change, does this prayer still have application today? I believe it must be as valid today as it was when it was first spoken. The nations and peoples that are currently pursuing the same destructive agenda,

---

The nations that want to see Israel destroyed are signing away their own future

---

place themselves in the same position as the nations and people of Jeremiah's day, and they will have to answer to God for those actions.

But in case you should think this is unfair, we should note that these nations also have a choice in their response. Speaking of the countries round about Israel, God says this: *"As for all my wicked neighbours who seize the inheritance I gave to My people Israel, I will uproot them from their lands and I will uproot the House of Judah from among them. But after I uproot them, I will again have compassion and will bring each of them back to his own inheritance and his own country. And if they learn well the ways of My people and swear by My name saying, 'As surely as the LORD lives'—then they will be established among My people. But if the nation does not listen, I will completely uproot and destroy it," declares the LORD.*[6]

But God's purposes for His people remain fixed. It is the Lord

5   Jeremiah 10:25
6   Jeremiah 12:14-17

who accepts responsibility for their ingathering. *"I Myself will gather the remnant of My flock out of the countries where I have driven them . . . they will be fruitful and increase in number."*[7] And there is yet more.

We have already seen that 'this day' occurs when Jesus, the Messiah, has come. It is not about a return from Babylonian exile, as some would have us believe, but about God's purposes in the end times. In Jeremiah twenty-three we read: *"The days are coming," declares the LORD, "when I will raise up to David a righteous branch . . . In His days Judah will be saved and Israel will live in safety. This is the Name by which He will be called: The LORD our Righteousness . . . the days are coming . . . when people will no longer say, 'As surely as the LORD lives, who brought the Israelites up out of Egypt,' but they will say, 'As surely as the LORD lives, who brought the descendants of Israel up out of the land of the north and out of all the countries where He had banished them.' Then they will live in their own land."*[8]

- Ultimately all Israel will live in safety
- A totally righteous man will come from the Davidic line
- He will be called *'The LORD our Righteousness'*
- The escape from Egypt will be forgotten as men praise God for bringing His people back from all the countries of the world

Remarkable words—remarkable prophecy! They are the words of God. The psalmist said: *'God is our refuge and our strength, a present help in time of trouble.'*[9] God is going to do a new thing among His people. It is something they will acknowledge as sovereignly ordained and planned. The first signs of it have been seen in the last sixty years. The most recent and obvious example has been the exodus of Jews from Russia. When Russia was a communist state the number

---

7   Jeremiah 23:3
8   Jeremiah 23:5-8
9   Psalm 46:1

of exiles allowed to return could almost be counted on the fingers of one's hands—now, despite difficulties, despite the need to bribe officials, despite the dangers involved to those providing transport, Jews have returned from Russia in vast numbers. These hundreds of thousands of people have returned from the land of the north before our very eyes.

A number of people sense this opportunity will not last, but God is always faithful to His promises. However He decides to fulfil them, they will come to pass. We are living in an age that has begun to see this happen, which should be an indication to us of how close we are to the end of the present world as we know it. We need to keep a watch on the global situation and read it in the light of scripture; neither exaggerating what is happening, nor ignoring it.

But the theme of restoration, seen so clearly in Isaiah, is found equally vividly in Jeremiah. God reaches out in mercy, even through their present judgement: *'I am with you and will save you,' declares the LORD. 'Though I completely destroy all the nations among which I scatter you, I will not completely destroy you. I will discipline you but only with justice; I will not let you go entirely unpunished . . . I will restore you to health and heal your wounds,' declares the LORD, 'because you are called an outcast, Zion for whom no-one cares.'*[10]

It is God who restores her, God who stands by her when all the nations despise her. As the present age continues, we hear politicians of all persuasions increasingly condemn Israel for intransigence. Even America, her closest ally in recent years, has started to adopt a far more ambivalent attitude in her dealings with the state of Israel. Is it any wonder that God then intervenes? Should that not cause us to fear for our own nations as they continue their arrogant and presumptive approach to this situation, a situation that has, at its heart, deep spiritual roots.

But God is not to be swayed: *The LORD appeared to us in the past, saying: "I have loved you with an everlasting love; I*

10   Jeremiah 30:11 and 17

have drawn you with loving-kindness. I will build you up again and you will be rebuilt, O virgin Israel" . . . *This is what the LORD says: "Sing with joy for Jacob; shout for the foremost of the nations. Make your praises heard, and say, 'O LORD, save Your people, the remnant of Israel.'* Jeremiah continues with these words from God: *See, I will bring them from the land of the north and gather them from the ends of the earth. Among them will be the blind and the lame, expectant mothers and women in labour; a great throng will return . . . Hear the Word of the LORD, O nations; proclaim it in distant coastlands: 'He who scattered Israel will gather them and will watch over His flock like a shepherd.' For the LORD will ransom Jacob and redeem them . . . I will turn their mourning into gladness; I will give them comfort and joy instead of sorrow."*[11]

"The time is coming," declares the LORD, "when I will make a new covenant with the House of Israel and with the house of Judah. It will not be like the covenant I made with their forefathers when I took them by the hand to lead them out of Egypt . . . This is the covenant I will make . . . I will put My law in their minds and write it on their hearts. I will be their God, and they will be My people . . . they will all know Me . . . I will forgive their wickedness, and will remember their sin no more."[12]

What is God's eternal view of Israel, as opposed to His temporary view of their need to be disciplined?

- God has loved them with an everlasting love
- God will build them up again
- God declares they are the foremost of the nations
- God will bring them from the ends of the earth
- God (who scattered Israel) will watch over them like a shepherd
- The Lord will ransom Jacob

---

11   Jeremiah 31:3 and 7-13 extracted
12   Jeremiah 31:31-34 extracted

- God will give them joy instead of sorrow
- God will make a new covenant with His people
- It will be in their minds and hearts
- They will all know God
- God will forgive all their wickedness

This is what the LORD says: "Sing with joy for Jacob; shout for the foremost of the nations. Make your praises heard and say, 'O LORD, save Your people, the remnant of Israel.' "

There are those (and we will return to them later) who claim that these promises refer to the church and to God's plans for the church. A simple, contextual examination of these verses shows this to be patently absurd. These scriptures are addressed to the house of Israel and Judah. The phrase is used repeatedly to ensure people understand it refers to both parts of the divided kingdom. It refers to those led out of Egypt; it refers to God forgiving their sin. As Christians, our sins have been forgiven through Jesus, the Messiah. Why then should there be a need for future forgiveness and a future new covenant for us? Do we not already have it? Of course we do!

Many people do not understand the promises given to God's people because they have never read God's Word thoroughly, or they have been poorly taught, or because they have not seen that scripture has literal and spiritual significance There are others, to whom a future for Israel is anathema. It sits uneasily with their view of a triumphant church which sorts out the world and hands it on, subdued, to Jesus. God's sovereign acts deny them a sense of their own importance.

When we walk that path we walk dangerously close to judgement. When we discover what God's purposes are we need to stand behind those purposes in prayer and look for them to come to pass in God's time. If we mistakenly oppose them we need to move ourselves into line with God's view, not expect God to move into line with our plans. A wrong sense of our own worth and value is as dangerous a path of delusion as having no sense of our own value and worth.

God is wholly consistent in His promises to eventually save and redeem His people, Israel.

In order that there should be no doubt about His intentions, God uses analogies taken from the natural world to reinforce His stated purposes for Israel: *He who appoints the sun to shine by day, who decrees the moon and stars to shine by night, who stirs up the sea so that its waves roar—the LORD Almighty is His name: "Only if these decrees vanish from My sight," declares the LORD, "will the descendants of Israel ever cease to be a nation before Me." This is what the LORD says: "Only if the heavens above can be measured and the foundations of the earth below be searched out will I reject all the descendants of Israel because of all they have done,"* declares the LORD. [13]

The promise of permanence is repeated two chapters later: *"This is what the LORD says, 'If you can break My covenant with the day and My covenant with the night, so that day and night no longer come at their appointed time, then My covenant with David My servant . . . can be broken and David will no longer have a descendant to reign on his throne. I will make the descendants of David My servant and the Levites who minister*

---

13   Jeremiah 31:35-37

before Me as countless as the stars of the sky and as measureless as the sand on the seashore.'" The Word of the LORD came to Jeremiah: "Have you not noticed that these people are saying, 'The LORD has rejected the two kingdoms He chose?' So they despise My people and no longer regard them as a nation. This is what the LORD says: 'If I have not established My covenant with day and night and the fixed laws of heaven and earth, then I will reject the descendants of Jacob and David My servant and will not choose one of his sons to rule over the descendants of Abraham, Isaac and Jacob. For I will restore their fortunes and have compassion on them.' "[14]*

The whole of creation is invoked as witness to God's pre-determined plans:

- Only if the sun and moon cease to exist will Israel cease to exist

- Only if day and night cease will Israel cease to exist

- Only if all space and all the oceans can be fully explored will Israel cease to exist

Those who dismiss the Word of God in the light of such emphatic declarations might as well join the fan club of King Canute—they are in danger of being swept away by God's revealed truth. They will not hold up God's plans, but they may drown trying to deny or oppose them. For ourselves, we need to wake up and not merely admire the language of these passages. If our creator, God, holds creation itself to task for the keeping of Israel, what an awesome promise that is.

So, as we finish this merest of glances at Jeremiah, a man who suffered so much and who lived through such a time of judgement and destruction, we have to acknowledge the recurrent theme we are finding in God's dealings with His people—God is wholly consistent in His promises to eventually save and redeem His people, Israel.

14   Jeremiah 33:20-26

Chapter 11

EZEKIEL AND THE VALLEY OF DRY BONES

"I will no longer hide My face from them, for I will pour out My Spirit on the House of Israel, declares the Sovereign LORD."

Ezekiel 39:29

If we thought that the tenor of Isaiah and Jeremiah was sombre and that we would surely not find anything to match it, Ezekiel is not the book to choose. Judgement after judgement thunder from the pages; warning after warning. Even while he spoke, Ezekiel's life was in almost constant danger, his words mocked and disregarded. I wonder how many Christians today would be so quick to claim for themselves the title of prophet if they understood what might happen to someone who genuinely speaks from God?

Having rebuked the priests and leaders of Israel for their lack of proper care of the people, God once more pronounces judgement against them. It will come as no surprise however, for us to find God's compassion for His people is never far from the surface. *"For this is what the Sovereign LORD says: I Myself will search for My sheep and look after them . . . I will bring them out from the nations and gather them from the countries, and I will bring them into their own land. I will pasture them on the mountains of Israel . . . I Myself will tend My sheep and make them lie down, declares the Sovereign LORD. I will search for the lost and bring back the strays. I will bind up the injured and strengthen the weak . . . I will shepherd the flock with justice.'*[1] Who is personally and intimately involved in all of this? It is God Himself.

Look how many times in this brief passage of scripture God speaks in the first person. Fifteen times between verse ten and verse sixteen we hear God say 'I'. How does God describe His people? They are:

- My sheep
- It is their own land
- God will tend (look after) them
- He will search for the lost
- He will bind up the injured
- He will strengthen the weak
- He will shepherd them with justice

But there appear to be others who have tried to muscle in on this land or have claimed a position God has not given them. As the chapter continues God warns those who have trampled the land, taken the best pasture, shoved with flank and shoulder and butted with horns. *I will judge between one sheep and another.*[2] God declares. Not only does this speak of those in Israel who lacked justice; it is a warning to us (particularly in the Western Church) who appropriate all the blessings of God for ourselves, while happily laying all the curses at the feet of the Jewish people. Distorting truth may create an illusion of reality, but it will ultimately be discovered to be false in the light of events.

In the following verse, Ezekiel is clearly speaking about the future when he says, *They will live in safety, and no-one will make them afraid. I (the Lord) will provide for them a land renowned for its crops, and they will no longer be victims of famine in the land or bear the scorn of the nations.*[3] Here is another prophetic scripture awaiting fulfilment, a promise

1   Ezekiel 34:11-16 extracted
2   Ezekiel 34:22
3   Ezekiel 34:28-29

God is still determined to keep.

As for the nations that attack Israel, the message for them is the same as that given through Isaiah and Jeremiah. *"Therefore prophesy concerning the land of Israel and say to the mountains and the hills, to the ravines and the valleys: 'This is what the Sovereign LORD says: "I speak in My jealous wrath because you have suffered the scorn of the nations. Therefore this is what the Sovereign LORD says: I swear with (My) uplifted hand that the nations around you will also suffer scorn.'"*[4]

"I will give you a new heart and put a new spirit within you; I will remove from you your heart of stone and give you a heart of flesh."

In contrast, God promises restoration for Israel. *"'But you, O mountains of Israel, will produce branches and fruit for My people Israel, for they will soon come home. I am concerned for you and will look on you with favour; you will be ploughed and sown, and I will multiply the number of people upon you, even the whole house of Israel. The towns will be inhabited and the ruins rebuilt . . . I will cause people, My people Israel, to walk upon you. They will possess you, and you will be their inheritance; you will never again deprive them of their children.'"*[5]

We will return to the theme of these verses later, but we note it is God who multiplies the people upon the land. Towns and cities will be inhabited and rebuilt and their children will dwell there. With the return of so many Jews to the land during the course of the twentieth century, we have seen that promise begin to come to pass. While the land lay in foreign hands, Jerusalem crumbled and the country lay desolate—

4   Ezekiel 36:6-7
5   Ezekiel 36:8-12

with the return of a Jewish majority the transformation has been astonishing.

In case anyone is still in any doubt as to why God does this, Ezekiel spells it out as he continues his exposition of the future: *'It is not for your sake, O House of Israel . . . but for the sake of My Holy Name . . . I will show the Holiness of My great Name, which has been profaned among the nations, the Name you have profaned among them. Then the nations will know that I am the LORD, declares the Sovereign LORD, when I show Myself Holy through you before their eyes.'*[6]

- It is not Israel who are holy, it is God

- God's name has been profaned among the nations

- The nations will recognise God's Holiness when God fulfils His Word to Israel

No excuses are offered for Israel. Israel has sullied God's name (as we can so often do as Christians, by careless discipleship or by flagrant disobedience to His Word). But God shows Himself Holy by restoring Israel to the land. I am baffled as to why so many sincere and outwardly enthusiastic Christians have such difficulty in accepting this fact. They seem to begrudge God's right to declare He still reigns among the nations. I can think of no more thrilling public acclamation of God to which the whole church can look, than the regathering of God's people, Israel.

This is no regathering fulfilled in history, but one we can see continuing before our own eyes. *"'For I will take you out of the nations; I will gather you from all the countries and bring you back to into your own land . . . I will give you a new heart and put a new spirit in you; I will remove from you your heart of stone and give you a heart of flesh. And I will put My Spirit in you and move you to follow My decrees and be careful to keep My laws. You will live in the land I gave your*

6   Ezekiel 36:22-23

forefathers; you will be My people, and I will be your God.'"[7] Let us list what their ultimate condition will be:

- They will have a new heart
- They will have a new spirit
- They will have a heart of flesh instead of stone
- God's Spirit will be within them
- They will be careful to keep God's laws
- They will live in the land
- They will be God's people
- God will be their God

Taken out of the nations, gathered from the ends of the earth, with a new heart and God's Spirit, God will change Israel! But it is only when God has brought them to this place that the people will *"loathe (*themselves*) for (*their*) sins and detestable practices."*[8] God acts first and that provokes the response. We have to look with spiritual eyes, not judge with earthly wisdom. After all, as Christians, we are reminded that God loved us when *we were dead* in our *transgressions and sins.*[9]

Following further reaffirmation of God's plans for Israel, we arrive at Ezekiel thirty-seven and the valley of dry bones. In one sense all passages of scripture are remarkable, but for graphic illustration this is truly extraordinary.

Led by the Spirit of God, Ezekiel found himself in a mountainous region, gazing at millions of bones, stretching over the valley floor, as far as the eye could see. There in that valley, chilling and awful in its introduction, God demonstrated Himself as the Lord of life and Creator of all living things. Ezekiel, asked if this army of bones could live, wisely replied, *"O Sovereign LORD, You alone know."*[10] God then called upon Ezekiel to prophesy to the bones, and in such a way that defied human logic and the witness of his own eyes. And this is what he was called to prophesy: *"'I will*

7   Ezekiel 36:24 and 26-28
8   Ezekiel 36:31
9   Ephesians 2:1
10 Ezekiel 37:3

make breath enter you, and you will come to life. I will attach tendons to you and make flesh come upon you and cover you with skin; I will put breath in you, and you will come to life. Then you will know that I am the LORD.'" [11] As Ezekiel prophesied, so those bones came together, flying around to make whole bodies! Flesh was put upon them, but there was still one more stage to go. Ezekiel was ordered to call to the wind that breath might enter into these slain, so that they might live.

What an astonishing picture this is of resurrection life. What a wonderful promise of what God had always intended for man and what a wonderful glimpse of what eternal life can be like, through the Messiah, Jesus Christ.

God explains to Ezekiel that these bones represent the whole House of Israel who say; *"Our bones are dried up and our hope is gone; we are cut off."*[12] Nonetheless, God tells us that even though that is how they see themselves, He is going to bring them back to Canaan. *"I will put My Spirit in you and you will live, and I will settle you in your own land."* [13] God's Word declares.

Not only will God do that, but He will also take the tribes and join them as one: *"'I will take the Israelites out of the nations where they have gone. I will gather them from all around and bring them back into their own land. I will make them one nation . . . they will never again be . . . divided into two kingdoms . . . They will be My people, and I will be their God . . . They and their children and their children's children will live there forever . . . I will make a covenant of peace with them; it will be an everlasting covenant . . . then the nations will know that I the LORD make Israel holy, when My sanctuary is among them forever.' "*[14]

Look at what God promises:

---

11   Ezekiel 37:5-6
12   Ezekiel 37:11
13   Ezekiel 37:14
14   Ezekiel 37:21-28 extracted

- Firstly, Israel will be one people. No longer the Southern or northern Kingdom, but a single nation as God intended.

- Secondly, they will live there forever. Fulfilment of this prophecy is taking place before our eyes. In prophecies of their temporary exile we do not find this phrase, so the prophecy to which this refers has not been capable of fulfilment until the present time.

- Thirdly, God makes a new and lasting covenant of peace with them at that time.

- Fourthly, God has His sanctuary among them forever, so that all nations will know that it is God who makes Israel holy.

It is obvious that the last of these promises has yet to be fulfilled. The progressive nature of the prophecy shows us that it will take place at the second coming of the Messiah— a time still to come. Therefore, if that is still to come, the promises God makes to Israel are for this present and future time, not for a past era, as some would argue.

". . . then the nations will know that
I the Lord make Israel holy, when
My sanctuary is among
them forever."

Who then, is to be included? Some, or all, of Israel? Let's see what Ezekiel says: *" . . . I will gather them to their own land, not leaving any behind. I will no longer hide My face from them, for I will pour out My Spirit on the house of Israel, declares the Sovereign Lord."*[15] Not only will God restore all of them to the land, His presence will bring the whole bounty of nature. *"Fruit trees of all kinds will grow on both*

15   Ezekiel 39:28-29

banks of the river. Their leaves will not wither, nor their fruit fail . . . Their fruit will serve for food and their leaves for healing."[16]Again, God's future plans include total restoration of blessing on the land itself.

This is not a battle of flesh and blood, but of intense spiritual warfare.

What is to be this land? It is an expanded version of the land that God had already promised to Abraham, Isaac and Jacob: *"On the north side it will run from the Great Sea by the Hethlon Road past Lebo Hamath to Zedad, Berothah and Sibraim (which lies on the border between Damascus and Hamath), as far as Hazer Hatticon, which is on the border of Hauran. The boundary will extend from the sea to Hazar Enan, along the northern border of Damascus, with the border of Hamath to the north. This will be the north boundary. On the east side the boundary will run between Hauran and Damascus, along the Jordan between Gilead and the land of Israel, to the eastern sea and as far as Tamar. This will be the east boundary. On the south side it will run from Tamar as far as the waters of Meribah Kadesh, then along the Wadi of Egypt to the Great Sea. This will be the south boundary. On the west side, the Great Sea will be the boundary to a point opposite Lebo Hamath. This will be the west boundary."*[17]

It is surely significant that God restates the borders of the land at the time of the future return of the Messiah. As we listen to the proposals of politicians and religious leaders concerning Jerusalem and Israel, let us remember God has not redrawn the map; it still exists according to the boundaries He has established. Not only that, but God has established Jerusalem

16   Ezekiel 47:12
17   Ezekiel 47:15-20

as a city whose name will be: *"THE LORD IS THERE."*[18]

What then can we conclude from our examination of Ezekiel? Will this great prophet contradict the message of Isaiah and Jeremiah? Shall we vote for judgement to triumph over mercy? Not if we read these passages in context? Not if we begin to open our eyes to the Holy Spirit and allow Him to show us the plans God has for His people and for the land they will one day inhabit fully.

Should we be surprised, in the light of this, if every step that inches Israel towards this goal is contested? This is not a battle of flesh and blood, but of intense spiritual warfare. We shouldn't be taken unawares. As we close the pages on Ezekiel, it is worth remembering the words of David, as he examined man's rule in the light of God's decisions:

Why do the heathen rage, and the people imagine a vain thing? The kings of the earth set themselves, and the rulers take counsel together, against the LORD, and against His Anointed, saying, Let us break Their bands asunder, and cast away Their cords from us. He that sitteth in the heavens shall laugh: The LORD shall have them in derision. Then shall He speak unto them in His wrath, and vex them in His sore displeasure. Yet have I set My King upon My holy hill of Zion. I will declare the decree: the LORD hath said unto Me, Thou art My Son, this day have I begotten Thee. Ask of Me, and I shall give the heathen for Thine inheritance, and the uttermost parts of the earth for Thy possession. Thou shalt break them with a rod of iron; Thou shalt dash them in pieces like a potter's vessel. Be wise now therefore, O ye kings: be instructed, ye judges of the earth. Serve the LORD with fear, and rejoice with trembling. Kiss the Son, lest He be angry, and ye perish from the way, when His wrath is kindled but a little. Blessed are all they that put their trust in Him. [19]

18   Ezekiel 48:35
19   Psalm 2 (Authorised Bible)

Chapter 12

DANIEL TO MALACHI: A PROPHETIC JOURNEY

"O Lord, in keeping with all Your righteous acts, turn away Your anger and Your wrath from Jerusalem, Your city, Your holy hill."

Daniel 9:16

Once again, it is worth stressing that we are not looking at scripture in detail as we examine these great men of God. Rather, we are glancing at some aspects of what God has revealed and promised concerning Israel. Therefore we need to remember that the scriptures that follow are representative, not exhaustive. Where better to begin than the book of Daniel.

DANIEL

Daniel's ministry, covering as it does a period of some seventy years, is perhaps best known for its outline of successive kingdoms and rulers who would bestride the world stage. For us, in our present study, it sews another thread into the tapestry of God's eternal purposes for mankind and for Israel.

'In my vision at night I looked, and there before me was one like a son of man, coming with the clouds of heaven. He approached the Ancient of Days and was led into His presence. He was given authority, glory and sovereign

power; all peoples, nations and men of every language worshipped Him. His dominion is an everlasting dominion that will not pass away, and His kingdom is one that will never be destroyed.[1] Daniel is referring, of course, to the reign of Jesus, the Messiah, elsewhere entitled the Lion of the tribe of Judah. The eternal kingdom has an eternal king. For Jewish believers in the Messiah and for Christians alike, this Old Testament confirmation of the Messiah's eternal rule is a guarantee of eternal, not temporal, life.

As well as the revelation of future events that were given to him, Daniel was very much grounded in the reality of the age in which he lived. Having understood from scripture that Israel's first exile would last seventy years, he came before God in prayer. The basis of his prayer was God's promise that He would be merciful to Israel and fulfil His Word to them. The requests are made, not with pride, but with contrition; not in anger, but with a sense of his own wrong-doing and the wrong-doing of the Jewish people. The practical challenge to our own journey of faith is very real. This is surely the way we should approach God; mindful of our own human weakness and frailty, seeing our utter reliance on the grace of God.

Daniel pleads with God: *"For Your sake, O Lord, look with favour on Your desolate sanctuary . . . We do not make requests of You because we are righteous, but because of Your great mercy. O Lord listen! O Lord forgive! O Lord, hear and act! For Your sake, O my God, do not delay, because Your City and Your people bear Your Name."*[2]

Daniel addresses God on the basis of the Lord's *'great mercy.'* He asks God to hear the groaning of the people and understand their predicament; then he asks God to look upon the city and see its desolation. He appeals to God on the basis of what is seen and he asks God to do three things:

---

1   Daniel 7:13-14
2   Daniel 9:17-19

- To listen

- To hear and act

- To not delay

Daniel's concern was with the return of Israel after the first exile, but the principles he applied are relevant to all requests we might make. When we come to God we need to have examined scripture for ourselves, in order to know how God wants us to pray. Daniel saw that God had a purpose for Israel that was ready to be fulfilled. He approached God on

---

> When we come to God we need to have examined Scripture for ourselves, in order to know how God wants us to pray.

---

the basis of the Lord's own promises. As we look at Israel today, we can see many further promises draw closer. We should be able to pray with conviction that God might act on behalf of His people, Israel.

We leave Daniel with a reminder that no empire, country or ruler can resist God's authority and not reap the consequences. King Nebuchadnezzar boasted of all that he had done. In direct response God humbled him and drove Nebuchadnezzar away from men so that he ate grass like cattle. When some time later God restored him to his senses and to his throne, Nebuchadnezzar uttered these words about the Lord; *His dominion is an eternal dominion; His kingdom endures from generation to generation. All the peoples of the earth are regarded as nothing. He does as He pleases with the powers of heaven and the peoples of the earth. No-one can hold back His hand, or say to Him, "What have you done?"*[3]

3   Daniel 4:34-35

If God can do that to the ruler of the greatest kingdom on earth at that time, He can surely do as He chooses in our day.

HOSEA

"I will ransom them from the power of the grave; I will redeem them from death. Where, O death, are your plagues? Where, O grave, is your destruction (sting)*?"*

Hosea 13:14

This opening scripture, taken from the penultimate chapter of Hosea, leads us once more to the voice of prophetic hope and deliverance we have encountered elsewhere. It is a verse that speaks of the promise of a Messiah and a hope for His people. But it is birthed out of the prophet's own heartfelt anguish.

Hosea was a prophet to Israel for about forty years, until approximately 715 BC, by which time Samaria had fallen. In human terms, no story in the Bible touches such deep chords of betrayal. It tells the story of Hosea, the man of utter faithfulness, and his anguish over his unfaithful wife, Gomer. It is an agony that echoes that of God's heart for His people, as they betray Him.

I agree with Campbell Morgan that the story is written as a memoir, so that Hosea marries in ignorance of what will unfold. Whether you hold that view, or the view that Hosea married his wife already knowing her character, makes no difference to the demonstration of God's love. This very human tragedy is ultimately transformed by a selfless act of undeserved redemption.

God called upon Hosea to name the children born to his wife Gomer, as expressions of what He was about to do to His people. Lo-Ruhamah and Lo-Ammi mean 'not loved' and 'not my people' respectively; a stark warning of God's view of the nation. Yet, even here God's compassion is never far from the surface, for in the verse after God has told them, *"I am not your God"* we read: *"Yet the Israelites will be like the sand on the seashore, which cannot be measured or counted. In the place where it was said of them, 'You are not My people'; they will be called 'sons of the living God'. The people of Judah and the people of Israel will be reunited, and they will appoint one leader and come up out of the land, for great will be the day of Jezreel. Say of your brothers, 'My people', and of your sisters, 'My loved one'.*[4]

Again punishment and judgement is ringed with an unquenchable love. God's heart for His people (as for us) looks to draw them back to Himself. Here too, lie further hints concerning our eternal salvation and the expansive nature of God's heart for mankind. The phrase *'sons of the living God'*, which we find here, is a constant theme of New Testament scripture, spoken to Jew and Gentile alike.

As for Israel's sin at this time; yes, it would be exposed, but no, God would not and could not let her go. One of the great hymns of the past speaks of our absolute hope in a 'love that will not me go'—such is God's love for His people.

How does God intend to arrest Israel, to gain her attention? Chapter two speaks of God's intention to lead her into the desert. To us that seems a remarkable idea; after all, a desert is a place of barrenness and discomfort, a place where one is stripped to the essentials, where possessions are far less important than survival.

But God plans it for a purpose, that very purpose of bringing Israel back to basics. *'"I will lead her into the desert and speak tenderly to her. There I will give her back her vineyards and will make the Valley of Achor a door of hope . . . I will betroth you to Me forever; I will betroth you in righteousness*

---

4 Hosea 1:10-11 and 2:1

and justice, in love and compassion. I will betroth you in faithfulness, and you will acknowledge the LORD *. . . I will plant her for Myself in the land; I will show My love to the one called 'Not My loved one'. I will say to those called 'Not My people', 'You are My people'; and they will say, 'You are my God.'"* [5]

Is there anywhere such a beautiful and poetic expression of the love of a father for his children? Man is incapable of arranging or contriving this; the initiative and execution is God's alone. It is God who:

- Betroths Israel to Himself forever
- Betroths her in righteousness and justice
- Betroths her in love and compassion
- Betroths her in faithfulness
- Plants her in the land
- Shows his love to her
- Declares they are His people

In a marriage service the bride and groom make vows to one another. Here is God Almighty, bowing the knee as it were, stooping to earth to make vows of betrothal, vows of righteousness, justice, love and compassion. God's vows to His people are the vows He seeks of us. Micah summarizes it thus: *He showed you, O man, what is good. And what does the* LORD *require of you? To act justly, and to love mercy and to walk humbly with your God."* [6]

Although God sees the prostitution of the land and the sins that keep separating them from Him, God also remembers finding Israel. *"When I found Israel, it was like finding grapes in the desert; when I saw your fathers, it was like seeing the early fruit on the fig-tree." God saw Israel as 'a spreading vine.'* [7] In chapter eleven, God compares Israel's first relationship with that of a father to his own offspring:

---

5   Hosea 2:14-15, 19-20 and 23
6   Micah 6:8
7   Hosea 9:10 and 10:1

"When Israel was a child, I loved him . . ."[8] As God remembers their calling, He recognises His own divine covenant with them.

How Hosea's own heart must have broken as he spoke these words. How his own heart must have identified intimately with God's as he remembered the early days of his marriage to Gomer. But as Israel had sold herself into prostitution, so had his wife, leaving her husband and children behind. And yet, prompted by the Lord, when Gomer had fallen to the place where no-one wanted her, when she had become a laughing stock among the people, Hosea had bought his wife back for fifteen shekels of silver (about half a day's wages) and he had taken Gomer back into his own home.

We can almost hear the passion in the prophet's heart as he cries out these words to God's people: *"How can I give you up, Ephraim? How can I hand you over, Israel? . . . My heart is changed within Me; all My compassion is aroused . . ."*[9]

Here is God Almighty, bowing the knee as it were, stooping to earth to make vows of betrothal; vows of righteousness, justice, love and compassion.

Once more we see God's unquenchable love for His people. We see the consistency of His love in the midst of their sin. We may marvel at it, we may feel that they don't deserve it, but we thank God for the grace of it. It is that same grace that allows us to call, 'Abba, Father', knowing that in the Messiah, Jesus, our sins have been blotted out; that for all our many and repeated failings God accepts us as fellow citizens of the commonwealth of Israel.

8   Hosea 11:1
9   Hosea 11:8

That endless, compassionate search for the lost is found echoing again as we come to the final verses of Hosea. *"I will heal their waywardness and love them freely . . . I will be like the dew to Israel; he will blossom like a lily . . . like a cedar of Lebanon he will send down his roots . . . His splendour*

> 'You will be true to Jacob, and show mercy to Abraham, as You pledged on oath to our fathers in days long ago.'

---

*will be like an olive tree . . . He will flourish like the corn . . . He will blossom like a vine . . . your fruitfulness comes from Me (*the Lord).*"*[10]

In Hosea chapter six God had spoken of His people's love being: *"like the morning mist, like the early dew that disappears."*[11] In contrast, God's dew brings fruitfulness, fertility and abundance. These are God's future plans for his people, plans that end in acceptance, not rejection. Hosea leaves us these words with which to remember this prophecy: *Who is wise? He will realise these things. Who is discerning? He will understand them.*[12] May we be wise and understand them.

JOEL

But the Lord will be a refuge for His people, a stronghold for the people of Israel.

Joel 3:16

Joel's words, written some 800 years before the birth of the Messiah, speak of coming judgement upon Judah, but the

---

10 Hosea 14:4-8 extracted
11 Hosea 6:4
12 Hosea 14:

scope of the book is far greater than that, dealing as it does with the final days of this present age.

Judah, God again intones in Joel, cannot escape judgement, but out of that time of judgement and out of the nations' responses to Israel's discomfort, God Himself will be roused . . . *The Lord will be jealous for His land and take pity on His people.*[13] God promises to repay His people *"for the years the locusts have eaten . . . never again will My (His) people be shamed . . . And afterward, I will pour out My Spirit on all people. Your sons and daughters will prophesy, your old men will dream dreams, your young men will see visions . . . And everyone who calls on the Name of the Lord will be saved; for on Mount Zion and in Jerusalem there will be deliverance . . ."*[14]

What do these scriptures show us?

- Israel are His people
- Israel is His land
- God will restore their prosperity
- God will fill them with His Spirit
- Everyone who calls on the name of the Lord will be saved

Messianic promise follows Messianic promise and of course, as Christians, we may take great encouragement from these verses for ourselves. But those who spiritualise the blessings and deny their physical reality, struggle with the Lord taking pity on *'His land'* and *'His people.'* It is inconvenient to their theology that the land and the people should be mentioned together. It is easy for the church to claim to be God's people and it correct to do so, but our churches are transparently not 'His land' and it is nonsense to suggest otherwise.

The regathering of Israel that Joel describes is not some calm, gentle act that we can watch from a distance. As the day

---

13   Joel 2:18
14   Joel 2:25,28 and 32 extracted

approaches when the Jewish Messiah, Jesus Christ, returns, we can expect to see more and more shaking in the physical and political world.

As the day approaches when the Jewish Messiah, Jesus Christ, returns, we can expect to see more and more shaking in the physical and political world

---

As for the nations who have interfered in this matter (and nowadays that appears to include most of the UN) Joel speaks in the severest terms: *"In those days and at that time, when I restore the fortunes of Judah and Jerusalem, I will gather all nations and bring them down to the Valley of Jehosophat (the valley of God's judgement). There I will enter into judgement against them concerning My inheritance, My people Israel, for they scattered My people and divided up My land."*[15] The theme is continued throughout the verses that follow: *The LORD will roar from Zion and thunder from Jerusalem; the earth and the sky will tremble. But the LORD will be a refuge for His people, a stronghold for the people of Israel. "Then you will know that I, the Lord your God, dwell in Zion, My holy hill. Jerusalem will be holy; never again will foreigners invade her . . . Judah will be inhabited forever and Jerusalem through all generations. Their bloodguilt, which I have not pardoned, I will pardon." The LORD dwells in Zion!*[16]

What will happen at this time?

- God will gather all nations
- He will judge them concerning the scattering of Israel
- He will judge them concerning dividing up the land

---

15   Joel 3:1-2
16   Joel 3:16,17,20 and 21

- Jerusalem and Judah will be inhabited forever
- Israel will receive pardon

God will call all nations and peoples on earth to account concerning Israel and He will enter into judgement against them. God Himself will be Israel's protector and He will deal with these nations in regard to their attitude towards His people. That event is still to take place. We need to be aware of it and prepared for it. Will we stand with God's counsel, or will we be swayed by the counsel and wisdom of the world and of this present age?

While Joel looks towards the future, his prophetic message stands firmly in the tradition of the prophets we have already examined—judgement is inevitable, but final redemption is assured.

AMOS

"I will plant Israel in their own land, never again to be uprooted from the land I have given them."

Amos 9:15

As we move from Joel to Amos, it is fascinating to note how exactly the language of Joel is echoed by Amos. Joel tells us: *'The LORD will roar from Zion and thunder from Jerusalem.'*[17] Having set the scene, Amos' account begins with these words: *"The LORD roars from Zion and thunders from Jerusalem."*[18] God is confirming His prophetic word.

The opening verses of Amos deal with God's judgements on Israel's neighbours. When we consider the current situation in the Middle East, we need to remind ourselves what judgements still stand over the nations around Israel. We have already read about these judgements elsewhere in scripture. If we believe God has to judge Israel we need to recognise that the nations

17   Joel 3:16
18   Amos 1:2

around them are still in grave danger of destruction.

As we turn to Israel herself, we find a recurrent theme of the Bible emerging—judgement on hypocritical religious ceremony. The Lord says: *"I hate, I despise your religious feast; I cannot stand your assemblies. Even though you bring Me burnt offerings and grain offerings, I will not accept them. Though you bring choice fellowship offerings, I will have no regard for them. Away with the noise of your songs! I will not listen to the music of your harps. But let justice roll on like a river, righteousness like a never-failing stream!"*[19]

God tells His people that he wants them to cleanse their hearts, not put on an outward show of religious ceremony. It is easy for us to look and say; 'Yes, how poor, how bad they were at serving God.' But are we so very different? I am grateful for many of the songs of praise and worship written over the last thirty years, yet it's all too easy for our so-called enlightened, charismatic worship to reflect the worship Israel brought–neither can more traditional songs escape!

We bring our praise in our own self-righteousness, in our own importance, in our own conviction that we have the truth that others don't have. But do we truly place righteousness at the centre of our lives? Is our justice (in social service schemes so many churches are adopting) God's justice, or our version of what the world offers? And when we bring the gospel, do we bring the whole truth of God's Word, or do we give people some sugar-coated delusion of salvation?

God wanted Israel to face the truth about their lives, not cast them off, so they might see their need for a Saviour and come to repent. When God showed Amos both locusts and fire devouring the land, God responded to Amos' plea for mercy. But then God showed Amos a plumb-line, and Amos understood that God had to impose just and right judgement. A plumb-line enables a builder to erect a structure that is straight and true, not out of angle. God was saying that judgement had

19   Amos 5:21-24

to apply to the Jewish nation: *"Look, I am setting a plumb-line among My people Israel; I will spare them no longer."*[20]

There are those who believe that whatever Jewish people do must be good–they are under as much of a delusion as those who believe everything Jews do is wrong. God has not altered the basis of salvation, which is in the Messiah only, Jesus Christ. What God has done, as the Bible teaches, is to reveal that a time is coming when the veil will be taken from their hearts, so that they may respond openly.

It takes real faith to believe God in the midst of circumstances that would seem to point to abandonment. God cannot abandon His promises and He cannot abandon His people.

In Amos, as in Joel, God's pre-determined course leaves Israel with hope for the future. *"The days are coming,"* declares the LORD, *"when the reaper will be overtaken by the ploughman and the planter by the one treading grapes . . . I will bring back My exiled people Israel; they will rebuild the ruined cities and live in them. They will plant vineyards and drink their wine . . . I will plant Israel in their land, never again to be uprooted from the land I have given them,"* says the LORD your God. [21]

- God will bring back His people
- They will rebuild the cities and live in them
- God will plant them in the land
- Never again will they be taken from it

20   Amos 7:8
21   Amos 9:13-15

At this time those still planting and reaping are overtaken by the ploughman and the one treading grapes. This has literal and spiritual meaning. God will pour out His Spirit in such a way that even as people are declaring God's Word and His promises, others will already be responding. This will be no slow growth (though there is no doubt it is laid on an existing foundation), it is much, much more. It is an ingathering that goes far beyond our human grasp, because God will be sovereignly and personally involved. Amos, like the prophets before him, is declaring Israel's final restoration at God's intervention.

OBADIAH

"... *On Mount Zion will be deliverance; it will be holy and the house of Jacob will possess its inheritance."*

Obadiah 17

Catch the pages of your Bible together and you will miss the twenty-one verses of Obadiah. The nation of Edom, who should have been Israel's natural allies, stood by and watched as Babylon invaded Israel. As a result of their actions, Obadiah warned the Edomites that their nation would cease to exist. For Israel however, there was still a future. *"But on Mount Zion will be deliverance; it will be holy and the house of Jacob will possess its inheritance."*[22]

Part of that inheritance is defined in verses nineteen to twenty-one: *'People from the Negev will inhabit the mountains of Esau, and people from the foothills will possess the land of the Philistines. They will occupy the fields of Ephraim and Samaria, and Benjamin will possess Gilead. This company of Israelite exiles who are in Canaan will possess the land as far as Zarephath; the exiles from Jerusalem that are in Sepharad will possess the towns of the*

---

22   Obadiah 17

Negev. Deliverers will go up on Mount Zion to govern the mountains of Esau. And the kingdom will be the LORD's.'[23]

The enemies of Israel will cease to exist. In *'the day of the LORD'* God will restore Israel for Himself. These verses cannot be 'spiritualised' away. As in the other prophetic books we have examined, we see God continues to be concerned for the land and the nation.

MICAH

"You will again have compassion on us . . . You will be true to Jacob, and show mercy to Abraham . . . "

Micah 7:19 and 20

Written in the eighth and seventh century BC, Micah spoke to both the Southern and Northern Kingdoms. The message he brought began with judgement; judgement on a people who had turned away from God, judgement on a people who were worshipping foreign gods and judgement on a people who had entered into alliances of which God did not approve. Samaria is to be *'a heap of rubble . . . her wound is incurable . . . disaster has come from the LORD, even to the gate of Jerusalem.'*[24]

But once more, alongside God's judgement on the present generation, we find God's future regathering. *"I will surely gather all of you, O Jacob; I will surely bring together the remnant of Israel. I will bring them together like sheep in a pen, like a flock in its pasture, the place will throng with people."*[25]

This is no casual regathering, no partial return. They are described as sheep in a pen. Now I don't know if you've ever been to a sheep market, but when you see sheep herded into pens there is little room left—all you see is a mass of sheep!

---

23   Obadiah 19-21
24   Micah 1:6,9 and 12 extracted
25   Micah 2:12

But they will also be like a flock in a pasture. My wife and I used to live in the country and often the fields around our house would be alive with the sounds of sheep. One fact becomes very obvious if you spend any time around sheep— you discover they are very curious. They always explore what they are given. The two descriptions together speak of fullness, of many people spreading out over the whole land; not a tiny remnant that will not be noticed. And in case we have missed the analogy Amos concludes: *'the place will throng with people.'* The return is extensive as God draws His people back to the land.

The picture of Israel, as a flock of sheep, is not accidental. In John's gospel we find the story of Jesus as the good shepherd. Jesus told those listening to Him; *"I am the good shepherd; I know My sheep and My sheep know Me—just as the Father knows Me and I know the Father—and I lay down My life for the sheep. I have other sheep that are not of this pen. I must bring them also."*[26]

What does this passage tell us:

- Jesus is the good shepherd
- Jesus knows His sheep (Israel)
- Israel will know Jesus
- Jesus will lay down His life for His people
- Jesus also has other sheep (Gentiles)
- He will include the Gentiles

Now I know Jesus used examples of everyday life to illustrate what he was talking about, but it is surely no accident that the New Testament so closely echoes this Old Testament image. It is not too much to suggest that Micah's picture once more hints at the coming Messiah, the Messiah we see so vividly revealed as Jesus in the passage from John.

Micah chapter three castigates the rulers of the time for their

26   John 10:14-16

abuses. It is because of these rulers that *'Jerusalem will become a heap of rubble'*[27] But almost immediately God returns to His favourite theme of final restoration: *In the last days the mountain of the LORD's temple will be established as chief among the mountains . . . Many nations will come and say, "Come, let us go up to the mountain of the LORD, to the house of the God of Jacob. He will teach us His ways . . . The law will go out from Zion, the Word of the LORD from Jerusalem."*[28]

It is apparent we are once more looking towards the Messianic reign of Jesus. Verses six and seven continue the theme: *"In that day," declares the LORD, "I will gather the lame; I will assemble the exiles and those I have brought to grief. I will make the lame a remnant, those driven away a strong nation. The LORD will rule over them in Mount Zion from that day and forever."*[29]

- The Lord's temple will be established (future tense)
- Many nations will go up to it
- It is the house of the God of Jacob (Israel)
- The Lord will teach these people
- The Word of the Lord will go out from Jerusalem
- The exiles will be regathered
- Those driven away will become a strong nation
- The Lord will rule over His people

Here the flowering of Messianic reign is seen by the whole world. In its midst is a restored Israel.

We leave Micah with a look at one further promise, a promise that concludes this great prophetic book: *You do not stay angry forever but delight to show mercy. You will again have compassion on us; You will tread our sins underfoot and hurl all our iniquities into the depths of the sea. You will be true to Jacob, and show mercy to Abraham, as You pledged on oath to our fathers in days long ago.*[30] Redemption and mercy

---

27   Micah 3:12
28   Micah 4:1-2 extracted
29   Micah 4:6-7
30   Micah 7:18-20

triumph over the temporary judgement of a generation.

HABAKKUK

"For the revelation awaits an appointed time; it speaks of the end and will not prove false."

Habakkuk 2:3

Habakkuk's view of events was coloured by all he saw around him. He couldn't understand why God didn't punish the wicked, then, when he saw that God would use the Babylonians to punish Israel, he couldn't understand that either. Why should God allow a nation as wicked as Babylon to be an instrument of judgement? God's response brings us face to face with the eternal nature of God's Word. Judgement would be meted out, but at the time of the Lord's choosing; restoration would take place, but at the time of God's determination: *"Write down the revelation . . . For the revelation awaits an appointed time; it speaks of the end and will not prove false. Though it linger, wait for it; it will certainly come and not delay."*[31]

Faced with situations where little of what God has promised appears to be happening, many of us, as twenty-first century Christians, tend to give up, dismiss it, or look for some alternative solution. It takes real faith to believe God in the midst of circumstances that would seem to point to abandonment. God cannot abandon His promises and He cannot abandon His people.

The Lord needed Habakkuk to understand that the times and the seasons are in God's hands. Once Habakkuk knew and understood that, he was able to believe God, even if he might not be the one to see its fulfilment. Once more the prophecy finishes on a note of Messianic hope and redemption, though

31   Habakkuk 2:2-3

the time is yet unseen. *'Though the fig-tree does not blossom, and there are no grapes on the vine, though the olive crop fails and the fields produce no food, though there are no sheep in the pen and no cattle in the stalls, yet I will rejoice in the LORD, I will be joyful in God My Saviour.'*[32]

ZEPHANIAH

"The LORD your God is with you. He is mighty to save. He will take great delight in you, He will quiet you with His love, He will rejoice over you with singing."

Zephaniah 3:17

Zephaniah begins with a word of all-encompassing judgement against mankind: *"I will sweep away everything from the face of the earth . . . I will sweep away both men and animals . . . "*[33] God thunders. God's anger is against Judah for following false gods, but it is also stretched out against the nations around: Philistia, Moab, Ammon, Cush and Assyria.

But out of judgement, as if by this time we should be surprised, once more comes mercy. Here, the mercy extends beyond Israel to other nations, a Messianic promise to bring people from 'every tribe, nation and people.' God will *'purify the lips of the peoples, that all of them may call on the name of the LORD.'*[34] The proud are excluded, but *'the meek and humble, who trust in the name of the LORD,'* will be there. *The remnant of Israel will do no wrong . . . they will eat and lie down and no one will make them afraid. Sing, O Daughter of Zion; shout aloud, O Israel! Be glad and rejoice with all your heart, O Daughter of Jerusalem. The LORD has taken away your punishment, he has turned back your enemy. The LORD, The King of Israel, is with you; never again will you fear any harm. On that day they will say to Jerusalem, 'Do not fear, O Zion; do not let your hands hang limp. The LORD*

32 Habakkuk 3:17
33 Zephaniah 1:2-3
34 Zephaniah 3:9

your God is with you, He is mighty to save. He will take great delight in you, He will quiet you with His love, He will rejoice over you with singing . . . I will rescue the lame, and gather those who have been scattered . . . At that time I will gather you; at that time I will bring you home. I will give you honour and praise among all the peoples of the earth when I restore your fortunes before your very eyes," declares the LORD.[35]

- God wants to save people from all nations

- Those who are humble and call to God will be saved

- God is the instrument of salvation

- It is God who is moved to gather them

- God who is moved to restore them

- God who brings them revelation

It is not the strong or the confident, but *'the lame'* and *'those who have been scattered.'* These are people for whom the Lord is their only hope. But God's heart is steadfast in this matter and He is acting as a covenant-keeping God for His people. It is that repeated refrain that takes us on to our final brief glance at the Old Testament, found in Zechariah.

ZECHARIAH

"And I will pour out on the house of David and the inhabitants of Jerusalem a spirit of grace and supplication."
Zechariah 12:10

Zechariah sits firmly in the mainstream of all we have been studying and details the return of the Messiah, the Lord Jesus, in far greater detail.

---

35 Zephaniah 3:13-20 extracted

In chapter one we find the angel of the Lord interceding with God, and asking how long mercy will be withheld from Jerusalem and the towns of Judah, and we find that God's response is to speak *'kind and comforting words to the angel . . . '*[36] who talked with Zechariah. The angel assures Zechariah that God is not indifferent to all that he sees. *"Proclaim this word: this is what the LORD Almighty says: 'I am very jealous for Jerusalem and Zion, but I am very angry with the nations that feel secure. I was only a little angry, but they added to the calamity . . . I will return to Jerusalem with mercy, and there My house will be rebuilt. And the measuring line will be stretched out over Jerusalem . . . Proclaim further: This is what the LORD Almighty says: 'My towns will again overflow with prosperity, and the LORD will again comfort Zion and choose Jerusalem.'"*[37]

What does this passage show us?

- God is very jealous for Jerusalem and Zion
- He is angry with the nations that have added to Jerusalem's calamity
- God will return to Jerusalem with mercy
- The towns will prosper
- The Lord will comfort Zion and choose Jerusalem
- God will stretch out his measuring line over Jerusalem

The measuring line is the same measuring line that God revealed to Amos, the measuring line of righteous judgement. All who busy themselves with Israel, who claim inheritance in Jerusalem, will have to stand against the plumb-line of God's Word—many will fail. God is *'very angry'* with the nations and people who have added to Jerusalem's calamity. Chapter two adds the stark warning: *"Whoever touches you* (Zion) *touches the apple of His (the* Lord's) *eye.*[38] Here is God not just as comforter and restorer, but defender.

36   Zechariah 1:13
37   Zechariah 1:14-17
38   Zechariah 2:8

As the Lord prophetically shows Zechariah what is to come, he sees an emerging picture of the Messiah's return. Though *'it may seem marvellous to the remnant of this people at that time'*[39] God has always intended it. God is *'determined to do good again to Jerusalem and Judah.'*[40] And that is but the beginning of it, for, as we have seen elsewhere, God is also determined to bless the Gentiles. *'And many peoples and powerful nations will come to Jerusalem to seek the LORD Almighty and to entreat Him.'*[41]

"In those days ten men from all languages will take firm hold of one Jew by the hem of his robe and say, 'Let us go with you, because we have heard that God is with you.'"[42] To me, this scripture strikes a chord with the picture of the sower overtaken by the reapers. Jewish people will be used in evangelism in a way that is beyond our comprehension. Instead of being jealous that this should happen, we should be happy. After all, wouldn't it be marvellous if ten men grabbed hold of every Christian and asked about God?

For Zechariah eight to become a reality, the Jewish nation need a revelation of Jesus as Messiah. God promises that this too will happen: *"And I will pour out on the house of David and the inhabitants of Jerusalem a spirit of grace and supplication. They will look on Me, the One they have pierced, and they will mourn for Him as one mourns for an only child, and grieve bitterly for Him as one grieves for a firstborn son."*[43] Revelation brings repentance and sorrow and that time will come.

As we read this passage of scripture, I cannot help but think how much we need the Holy Spirit to cause us to mourn as we come to Jesus: for us to realise what our sin is really like, to understand the pain and grief our selfishness causes God. When we pray that God may do this among His people, let's make sure we're willing to ask God to do it among us.

As this great prophetic book comes to a climax, danger signal

39   Zechariah 8:6
40   Zechariah 8:14
41   Zechariah 8:22
42   Zechariah 8:23
43   Zechariah 12:10

after danger signal flash out for the nations that seek to destroy Israel. God warns that He; *'will set out to destroy all the nations that attack Jerusalem.'*[44] God is going to gather the nations

---

'This is what the Lord Almighty says: "My towns will again overflow with prosperity; and the Lord will again comfort Zion and choose Jerusalem."'

---

together to Jerusalem *'to fight against it . . . Then the LORD will go out and fight against those nations, as He fights in the day of battle. On that day His feet will stand on the Mount of Olives, east of Jerusalem, and the Mount of Olives will split in two . . . Then the LORD my God will come, and all the holy ones with Him . . . The LORD will be King over the whole earth. On that day there will be one LORD, and His Name the only Name.'*[45]

What will happen at that time?

- The Lord will physically fight the nations
- He will stand on the Mount of Olives
- The Lord will be King over the whole earth
- All other gods will be destroyed

Once more we need to realise we are dealing here with God's absolutes. God will intervene in a manner that is beyond human comprehension. We speak glibly of weapons of mass warfare and we have a picture of the destruction man wreaks, but it pales into insignificance compared with the power and authority of God. We see hints of it in the Old Testament as we read of the destruction of Sodom and Gomorrah, the overthrow of Pharaoh's army and the destruction of

44   Zechariah 12:9
45   Zechariah 14:1-9 extracted

Sennacherib's forces by God, but it is an awesome and sobering thought that God will shake the earth in this way.

It is that note and prophecy that propels us towards the New Testament, for us to find out if God still has the same message to share, concerning Israel, when Jesus comes to the earth.

Chapter 13

FROM THE OLD TO THE NEW: THE GOSPELS

"The Lord God will give Him the throne of His father David, and He will reign over the house of Jacob forever; His kingdom will never end."

Luke 1:32-33

We left the Old Testament with the prophetic message of hope for Israel firmly established. Now, after a gap of some four hundred years, when we find no recorded Word of God, we come to the time when Jesus was born. Our purpose is not to trace an outline of Jesus' life through these pages, but it is to examine whether the gospels tie in with the promise of a Messiah as given in the Old Testament. Is the one born 'King of the Jews' the legitimate ruler of Israel?

The gospel of Matthew begins with the genealogy of Christ, running from Abraham, Isaac and Jacob (the patriarchs), through David, Solomon and their descendants of the kingly line, ending with Joseph, the husband of Mary. *Thus there were fourteen generations in all from Abraham to David, fourteen from David to the exile in Babylon, and fourteen from the exile to the Christ.*[1]

Luke also deals with the ancestry of Christ, tracing it back to God's creation of Adam. From Adam we move down through the family line until we arrive at Enoch (a man who did not see death), Noah (who brought his family through the flood),

---

1 Matthew 1:17

then once more through the patriarchs until we arrive at King David. From there the family line, though still traced back to David, separates from Solomon, eventually arriving at Heli, the father of Mary.

Why mention the genealogy? What relevance does it have to us? Well, instead of whizzing past family trees in the Bible, every time we come to read them, these lists should encourage us. They should encourage us because we find both Mary and Joseph able to trace their ancestry back through the royal line. The Holy Spirit was, of course, the One who caused Mary to give birth, but both she and Joseph could trace their lineage directly to David, and it was from David's line that the Jewish people knew the Messiah would come. Not only that, but this family tree shows us how Christ is to be prophet, priest and king. It is worth noting that whatever else the scribes and pharisees felt able to challenge Jesus on, they never once disputed His ancestry.

For those interested in genealogy, records of their ancestors are fascinating. For Christians, adopted as sons and daughters through the promises of the New Testament, there should be more than passing interest in the family into which they are adopted.

What then, do the disciples' accounts tell us about Jesus as Ruler and Saviour? In Matthew's gospel we are told that the angel came to Joseph, telling him not to be afraid: *"Take Mary home as your wife because what is conceived in her is from the Holy Spirit. She will give birth to a Son, and you are to give Him the name Jesus, because He will save His people from their sins."*[2]

We learn three things from this simple statement:

- God is involved in the birth
- He is to be called Jesus, meaning 'the Lord saves'
- His people will be saved from their sins

2   Matthew 1:20-21

The logical question to ask is—who are the people to whom the angel is referring? In the context of this passage, they are the Jewish nation. For those not convinced by a single scripture reference, further explicit examples exist throughout the New Testament. The first of these is provided in Matthew chapter two.

King Herod was disturbed by the visit of men from the east who had come saying: *"We have come to worship* (the one) *who has been born King of the Jews."*[3] As a result Herod sent for the religious leaders and asked them where the Christ, the Messiah, was to be born. Quoting from Isaiah they told him: *"'But you, Bethlehem, in the land of Judah, are by no means least among the rulers of Judah; for out of you will come a ruler who will be the shepherd of My people Israel.'"*[4]

The passage containing these brief words tells us much more about God's plan for Israel:

- Firstly, we see that Herod was disturbed by these reports and took them seriously, rather than dismissing them out of hand

- Secondly, Herod was sufficiently aware of prophecy to have heard about the possibility of a Messiah

- Thirdly, the religious leaders were also aware of God's promise to send a Messiah

- Fourthly, these same religious rulers had a clear understanding of the area from which the Messiah, Jesus, would come

- Fifthly, they understood (from their reading of Isaiah) that the one who came would be both the ruler and shepherd of Israel

The seriousness with which Herod took this information is seen later in Matthew two. *When Herod realised that he had been outwitted by the Magi, he was furious, and he gave orders to kill*

---

3   Matthew 2:2
4   Matthew 2:6 ibid Isaiah 7:14

all the boys in Bethlehem and its vicinity who were two years old and under, in accordance with the time he had learned from the Magi.[5] We can be sure that what stirred Herod in the physical realm, was a pale reflection of what was stirring in the spiritual realm, as the Messiah lived his early years.

Of the other gospel writers, Mark and John spend little time on the birth of Jesus, but Luke looks even more closely at the birth than does Matthew. We have already read Matthew's report of what the angel told Mary. Here, in Luke, we find this additional conversation: *"You will be with child and give birth to a son, and you are to give Him the name Jesus. He will be great and will be called the Son of the Most High. The Lord God will give Him the throne of His father David, and He will reign over the House of Jacob forever; His kingdom will never end."*[6]

In affirming the Messiah's legitimacy, the angel declares that Jesus is:

- The Son of the Most High (God the Father)
- That God will establish Him on David's throne
- That He will reign over the House of Jacob (Israel) forever
- That Jesus' kingdom will never end

So already, in the New Testament, we see God's plans for Israel gaining even sharper focus, not being tossed aside as some would like to suggest.

In the Anglican Church in England, the Nunc Dimittis is still sung at evensong. It includes the words: *"For my eyes have seen Your salvation, which You have prepared in the sight of all people, a light for revelation to the Gentiles and for glory to Your people Israel."*[7] These are of course the words of that lovely old saint of God, Simeon, on seeing Jesus in his parents' arms. They confirm what we have read elsewhere about Jesus, but they also add two further significant details:

- Firstly, we see that God has now brought His salvation

5   Matthew 2:16
6   Luke 1:31-33
7   Luke 2:30-32

to all mankind through Jesus, who is *'a light for revelation to the Gentiles'*

- Secondly, Simeon declares that Jesus will be for *'glory to Your people Israel'*

So we see that the purposes of God have not changed. What was implicit in the Old Testament is now made explicit in the New. The Gentiles are offered a new and living way to God. Israel, God's people, will see the glory of the Lord upon them. If, as some would say, there is now no Israel, why does Jesus, the Messiah, bring to the human stage both revelation and glory; the first for us as Gentiles, the second for Israel as His people? I can only conclude God does it because He is utterly faithful to His promises and His pre-determined will. We should be glad of the revelation that has been given us, not jealous over coming glory for Israel.

If, as some would say, there is now no Israel, why does Jesus, the Messiah, bring to the human stage both revelation and glory; the first for us as Gentiles, the second for Israel as His people?

'But surely,' these same people chorus, 'the Jews rejected Jesus as Messiah.' Really? I find such comments remarkable. Let's consider one incident from Matthew's gospel, the parable of the sower. The disciples were curious as to why Jesus spoke to the people in parables. Jesus explained that these are people who are *"ever hearing but never understanding."*[8] 'Ah, there you are!' cry the critics of the Jews. 'Rejection! Proved and absolute!' But let

8   Matthew 13:14 ibid Isaiah 6:9

us not be so hasty. Let us put the explanation in context. If we read on, we discover Jesus continues with these words: *"But blessed are your eyes because they see, and your ears because they hear."*[9] Who are those who have ears that hear? They are, of course, the disciples. Now it seems to escape the notice of those who reject Jewish claims to Jesus as Messiah, that Jesus is talking to a Jewish audience, who saw, heard and believed what He said.

Even a cursory glance at the gospels leaves no doubt that Jesus intended His message for a Jewish audience. It was to them He came and it was to them He entrusted the task of spreading the gospel to their fellow Jews and to the Gentile world. Although Jesus healed individuals who were not Jewish, He made it plain that His primary purpose while still on earth was to the house of Jacob. In Matthew fifteen Jesus declared: *"I was sent only to the lost sheep of Israel."*[10]

Towards the end of His time on earth, Jesus began to teach the disciples about what would happen after His resurrection. We find the account, with the same emphasis, in three of the gospel stories; Matthew, Mark and Luke. This is what Jesus told the disciples, as recounted in Luke: *"Watch out that you are not deceived. For many will come in My name, claiming, 'I am he,' and 'the Time is near.' Do not follow them. When you hear of wars and revolutions, do not be frightened. These things must happen first, but the end will not come right away."* Then He said to them: *"Nation will rise against nation, and kingdom against kingdom. There will be great earthquakes, famines and pestilences in various places, and fearful events and great signs from heaven."*[11]

Jesus makes it clear there is an ordered sequence to these events. In the scriptures that follow verse eleven, He tells the disciples they will suffer persecution. Some of them will be put to death. All of this was tragically fulfilled in the years that followed, as they discovered the human cost of being a disciple of Jesus.

Jesus also warns of the coming destruction of Jerusalem,

9   Matthew 13:16
10 Matthew 15:24
11 Luke 21:8-11

which we know took place in 70 AD. Those who remembered and recognised the warnings of Jesus were able to flee when the Romans temporarily lifted the siege. Those who were left found themselves facing the final assault and the total destruction of the temple. We can therefore agree the authenticity of the prophecy, as we have historical evidence of the facts.

Jesus went on to prophesy that after the Jews were taken as prisoners to all nations, *"Jerusalem (*would*) be trampled on by the Gentiles, until the times of the Gentiles are fulfilled."*[12] From that time, until the Six Day War of 1967, Jerusalem was never under the control of the Jewish nation. Indeed, that nation ceased to exist to all intents and purposes until 1947, when the right to once more call a part of the Promised Land by the name Israel, was recognised by the UN.

What conclusions may we draw from the astounding synopsis of history that Jesus presents?

- Jesus was not promising physical and military peace to his disciples at that time. Jesus did not want the disciples wondering why there was still evil in the world. He wanted them to teach the church that they would live in a world where there would be war and revolution. This is an important consideration for us when we are asked to pray for world peace. If God has said, through the Messiah, Jesus Christ, that we will not have peace, what are we praying for when we pray for world peace? If we are praying in a manner contrary to the will of God, we are at best deluding ourselves, but more probably opening ourselves up to wrong spiritual influences, which will affect our thinking on a range of issues.

- Jesus warned the disciples Israel was about to suffer judgement and persecution. Here we find Jesus walking in the tradition of Isaiah, Jeremiah and the

12 Luke 21:24

other prophets of the Old Testament.

- Many of the early disciples would be persecuted. Some disciples would be killed for putting their faith in Jesus as Messiah

- Israel's ancient capital city, Jerusalem, would come under foreign control until God decreed that the time for foreign domination was over

- Many people would come, claiming to be the Christ or claiming to have revelation from God. The false messiahs and false religions that have proliferated since Jesus' death bear ample testimony to the truth of this prophecy.

Jesus warned the disciples Israel was about to suffer judgement and persecution.

Jesus presented this message to a Jewish audience. In line with the Old Testament prophets he was outlining God's present and future plans for His people. As He continued he brought His disciples a vision of the final years of the world as it presently is: *"There will be signs in the sun, moon and stars. On the earth, nations will be in anguish and perplexity at the roaring and tossing of the sea. Men will faint from terror, apprehensive of what is coming on the world, for the heavenly bodies will be shaken. At that time they will see the Son of Man coming in a cloud with power and great glory. When these things begin to take place, stand up and lift up your heads, because your redemption is drawing nigh."*[13]

Given the sequential nature of Jesus' words, it is safe to assume that this latter part of prophecy could only take place once Israel had returned to the land. While the passage

---

13   Luke 21:25-28

encompasses a period of time, the emergence of the State of Israel in 1948, and the re-unification of Jerusalem under Jewish control, in 1967, means we have now moved into the age where these events will take place. We should, therefore, not be surprised to see greater physical upheaval on the earth than has been recorded before.

A recent insurance industry audit reported that large-scale natural disasters were three times as common now as they were in the 1960s. Some insurance experts claim that the rising rates of natural disasters are making parts of the world virtually uninsurable. As Christians however, we should remember the words of Jesus: *'Stand up and lift up your heads, for your redemption is drawing nigh.'*

We already know that Jesus spoke these words to a gathering of Jewish disciples. The promise of redemption is therefore not for the church alone, but a promise of redemption for Israel by their Messiah. It confirms the promises made in the Old Testament to Abraham, Isaac and Jacob—and their descendants after them!

At His death, Jesus, the Messianic servant, made the ultimate sacrifice for all the people, as their prophet, priest and king.

The death and resurrection of Jesus are well known to Christian and non-Christian alike and are found in detail in all four gospels. In the context of our journey through God's Word, five points are worthy of note:

- The conduct of the trial was illegal under both Jewish and Roman law
- Jewish and Roman regional leaders were complicit in

its execution

- When Pilate saw the people would not let Jesus go, he washed his hands in front of them and told them they would be responsible for what happened. *All the people answered, "Let His blood be on us and on our children!"*[14]

- When Jesus was crucified, He uttered this prayer to His Father: *"Father, forgive them, for they do not know what they are doing."*[15]

- *Pilate had a notice prepared and fastened to the cross. It read: JESUS OF NAZARETH, THE KING OF THE JEWS.*[16] Though the Jewish rulers objected, Pilate refused to change it.

We have to ask which is the greater; the prayer of Jesus for forgiveness or the cry of the mob for blood?

For those who argue that the Jews alone bear responsibility for Jesus' death, the historical information demonstrates otherwise. For those who produce the more convincing argument that the Jews brought a curse of bloodguilt down upon themselves, we have to ask which is the greater; the prayer of Jesus for forgiveness or the cry of the mob for blood? The answer, I trust, is obvious. The New Testament parallels the Old, and even while future judgement had been spoken on the generation to whom Jesus came, the cry for mercy and compassion had gone from the heart of the Son to the throne of the Father.

As for the title given to Jesus, if it was ironic, as some would have us believe, we have to ask why it so offended the Jewish

14   Matthew 27:25
14   Luke 23:34
16   John 19:19

leaders? It was a prophetic demonstration of Jesus as He would one day appear to the entire Jewish nation, *'great David's greater son.'* So, at his death, Jesus, the Messianic servant, made the ultimate sacrifice for all the people, as their prophet, priest and king.

Chapter 14

ACTS: THE BIRTH OF THE CHURCH

"From this man's descendants God has brought to Israel the Saviour Jesus, as He promised."

Acts 13:23

The gospels record a series of events in the days after Jesus' resurrection, when he appeared to the disciples, comforting, encouraging and teaching them, in preparation for the time when they would be taking the message of forgiveness of sins to the people and nations all around them.

Even though the scriptures about the Messiah's death now made much more sense to them, they were still puzzled about what was going to happen next. From their understanding of the Old Testament prophets, they knew that one day God would restore Israel to a place of prominence on the world stage. Naturally enough, following the miracle of Jesus' resurrection, they wanted to know if the kingdom would be restored to Israel at that time. In Acts we discover them asking Jesus that very question. Jesus replied: *"It is not for you to know the times or dates the Father has set by His own authority. But you will receive power when the Holy Spirit comes upon you; and you will be My witnesses in Jerusalem, and in all Judea and Samaria, and to the ends of the earth."*[1]

There are a number of conclusions we can draw from the response of Jesus to this question:

1   Acts 1:7-8

- The first was that Jesus understood their concern. Would God fulfil His promise to Israel and restore the nation? Now, if restoration was not going to take place, do you not think Jesus would have corrected their error? He could (indeed should) have corrected the idea of a sovereign Jewish State if it was not going to happen. Jesus' silence on the matter implicitly acknowledged Israel's future, while making it clear to the disciples that they should not become pre-occupied with the timing of that restoration.

If God had finished with Israel, if God had rejected His people; it surely was remarkable that the first people to whom the disciples presented the gospel were all Jewish.

- Secondly, it indicates that while we may see signs of the Messiah's second coming, it is God who decides the timing as and when He chooses.
- Thirdly, Jesus made it clear that these Jewish disciples were the ones who would take this universal gospel, first to their fellow Israelites and then to the ends of the world. If God had finished with Israel, if God had rejected His people; it surely was remarkable that the first people to whom the disciples presented the gospel were all Jewish. Only someone acting like an ostrich with their head in the sand could hope to avoid the obvious conclusion that God had not set aside the covenant with the patriarchs. The new covenant, the covenant of grace, was not a covenant of further

- separation, but a covenant of greater ingathering among all nations echoing the promise of the Old Testament.

- Fourthly, if God wanted the disciples to be witnesses of a new covenant, it implied that the Old covenant had limitations. Israel could never really draw close to God by observing the law. It had become apparent through history that the law showed up their sin for what it really was—always with them.

  As the apostle John put it, *the law was given through Moses; grace and truth came through Jesus Christ.*[2] It was in the wholly unmerited grace of Jesus that the seeds of redemption for the whole nation were sown.

With that as background, we arrive at the day of Pentecost. This is a day the Christian church celebrates as a time when God visited His power upon His people. It is to a crowd of *God-fearing Jews from every nation under heaven*[3] that this message is given, and it is upon them that the Holy Spirit is first poured out. Far from being cast off, the first truly successful evangelistic rally prompted an incredible response among those assembled Jews. Convicted by Peter's preaching: *Those who accepted his message were baptised, and about three thousand were added to their number that day.*[4] The first Christian church, though as yet not called by that title, is entirely Jewish. Has judgement triumphed over mercy in this new dispensation, or has mercy triumphed over judgement?

What then, happened to this early church that met in Jerusalem? The verses that follow tell us, painting a silent rebuke of the western church's so-called fellowships of today. *They devoted themselves to the apostles' teaching and to the fellowship, to the breaking of bread and to prayer . . . many wonders and miraculous signs were done by the apostles. All the believers were together and had everything in common . . .*

2   John 1:17
3   Acts 2:5
4   Acts 2:41

every day they continued to meet . . . they broke bread in their homes and ate together with glad and sincere hearts . . . And the Lord added to their number daily those who were being saved.[5] Cast off by God? I hardly think so.

The gospel was spread by Jews to the furthest corners of the known world.

Now, as in the days of the prophets, the disciples found themselves opposed by men who didn't want to hear their message, but even arrest and imprisonment were not sufficient to prevent them speaking out about Jesus as the Messiah of Israel. Eventually, as more and more men, women and children joined the disciples, the influence they were having among the Jewish population became so great that the Sanhedrin wanted to put the apostles to death. Persuaded this would be unwise, they instead had them flogged and ordered them not to speak in the name of Jesus. Did this cause them to cower away as they had hidden before the day of Pentecost? On the contrary, Acts reports: *The apostles left the Sanhedrin, rejoicing because they had been found worthy of suffering disgrace for the Name. Day after day . . . they never stopped preaching and proclaiming the good news that Jesus is the Christ.*[6]

But from then on they had no doubt that the religious leaders would look for an excuse to put them to death. Acts chapter seven records the first martyrdom among that early church, when Stephen is stoned to death. His response, even as the mob is stoning him, recalls the words of Jesus on the cross: *"Lord, do not hold this sin against them." When he had said this, he fell asleep.*[7] Mercy and love are still being extended,

---

5 Acts 2:42-47 extracted
6 Acts 5:41-42
7 Acts 7:60

even in the face of unreasoning hatred.

There are four consequences to this action:

- Firstly, *On that day, a great persecution broke out against the church at Jerusalem . . .*[8]

- Secondly, *all except the apostles were scattered throughout Judea and Samaria . . .*[9]

- Thirdly, Saul *began to destroy the church . . . he dragged off men and women and put them in prison.*[10]

- Fourthly, this persecution backfired on the religious authorities for *Those who had been scattered preached the word wherever they went.*[11]

Tragedy befalls the early Church, yet out of this God uses those same Jewish believers to take the Word of God across the whole region. We may logically presume that if these men and women were so willing to speak out about Jesus, the Jews who heard Peter on the day the Church was first born were equally bold. They were from all the nations, so the gospel was spread by Jews to the furthest corners of the known world. A Jewish people preaching about a Jewish Messiah and about a future hope for Israel.

But if there is hope for the Jewish community, what hope is there for us as Gentiles? Remarkably, despite his determined effort to prove himself a loyal servant to the Pharisees, Saul, the man we find persecuting the Church in Acts chapter eight, is confronted by a revelation of Jesus. Unable to see for three days, he is anointed by Ananias, who has been told by the Lord that Saul *"is My chosen instrument to carry My name before the Gentiles and their kings . . ."*[12] God is bringing to the stage of history, a man who is going to spearhead a mission that will see Christianity move beyond its Jewish roots and become established among the Gentile nations, building on the seeds already sown by the scattered Jewish believers.

8   Acts 8:1
9   Acts 8:1
10   Acts 8:3
11   Acts 8:4
12   Acts 9:15

And so, throughout the rest of Acts, Paul takes centre stage. He recognises Peter's primary calling to the Jewish people and his own to the Gentiles but, wherever he goes, he always presents the gospel to the Jews as well. Not always accepted by these communities, he nonetheless persists with his message until we find him, at the end of Acts, under house arrest at Rome. But while Paul may be physically confined, nothing can stop him declaring the truth about the Messiah. *Boldly and without hindrance he preached the Kingdom of God and taught about the Lord Jesus Christ.*[13]

13   Acts 28:31

Chapter 15

ROMANS: ISRAEL'S INHERITANCE REVEALED

As far as the gospel is concerned, they are enemies on your account; but as far as election is concerned, they are loved on account of the patriarchs, for God's gifts and His call are irrevocable.

Romans 11:28

At the end of Acts, we left Paul under house arrest in Rome. Before he ever arrived there, he wrote to the church at Rome, a church that had been planted by faithful disciples, as at that time none of the apostles had even visited the city. While the letter to the Roman church has wider significance, our chief concern is with Paul's outline of God's plans for Israel, contained in chapters nine to eleven.

The ninth chapter begins with Paul's expressed sorrow over the present state of his fellow Jews, before he paints a vivid picture of their Biblical inheritance: *Theirs is the adoption as sons; theirs the divine glory, the covenants, the receiving of the law, the temple worship and the promises. Theirs are the patriarchs, and from them is traced the human ancestry of Christ, who is God over all, for ever praised! Amen*[1]

What then do the Jews possess?

* Adoption
* Glory
* Covenants
* The law

1 Romans 9:4-5

- Temple worship
- The promises
- The patriarchs

All these are part of their heritage and as such are a part of their inheritance. To these seven he adds an eighth, which we have already examined—the human ancestry of Christ. The inclusion of Gentile believers into God's family comes through the Jewish Messiah, Jesus. It is through their journey over those thousands of years before Christ's birth that we find ourselves accepted into *the commonwealth of Israel.*[2]

As in the Old Testament, God does not want there to be any confusion over the group from whom this nation comes. *"It is through Isaac that your offspring will be reckoned"* . . . *it is the children of the promise who are regarded as Abraham's offspring . . . It does not therefore, depend on man's desire or effort, but on God's mercy.*[3]

It is not only through Abraham but specifically through Isaac, the child of the promise, that the New Testament defines the people entitled to call themselves Israel, the nation chosen by God.

This brings us to one of the great conundrums for the human mind, God's fore-ordained purposes. Paul reminds us of God's words to Moses; *"I will have mercy on whom I have mercy, and I will have compassion on whom I have compassion."*[4] But Paul emphasises that in all this God exercises justice. Even though man may not always understand it, through faith in Christ Jesus each individual may claim it.

Having reiterated that for the Gentiles there can be a *righteousness that is by faith,*[5] Paul tackles the heart of the dilemma behind the Jewish religion, the pursuit of righteousness by works, a process doomed to repeated failure. The problem Paul sees is that the zeal of the Jews is not based on knowledge of God, but on a list of rules and

2   Ephesians 2:12 (KJV)
3   Romans 9:7,12 and 16 extracted
4   Romans 9:15
5   Romans 9:30

regulations which have become centred in man, not the Lord. This prompts him to almost cry out from the page: *Brothers, my heart's desire and prayer to God for the Israelites is that they may be saved.*[6]

It is not only through Abraham but specifically through Isaac, the child of the promise, that the New Testament defines the people entitled to call themselves Israel, the nation chosen by God.

The solution, on the surface, is simple, as outlined in the first half of Romans ten: *"Everyone who calls on the Name of the Lord will be saved". . . if you confess with your mouth, "Jesus is Lord," and believe in your heart that God raised Him from the dead, you will be saved.*[7] But for the Jewish people there is a dilemma. They need to hear the Word, they need to hear the message, and they need those who will bring the message. Yet despite all this, and despite the fact that the early church was Jewish in initiation and constitution, the majority of Jews did not respond. Why was this?

It is, Paul explains, a question of the stupor that God has allowed to be placed upon them. Two questions follow from this: Firstly, why has God allowed this? Secondly, is this a situation in which there is no hope for Israel? We find our answer in Romans eleven where Paul mounts an emphatic rebuttal of Israel's rejection.

Again I ask: Did they stumble so as to fall beyond recovery? Not at all! Rather, because of their transgression, salvation has come to the Gentiles to make Israel envious. But if their transgression means riches for the world, and their loss

---

6 Romans 10:1
7 Romans 10:13 and 10:9

means riches for the Gentiles, how much greater riches will their fullness bring![8]

What does this passage tell us?

- Israel's sin has allowed salvation to come to the Gentiles
- This will make Israel envious
- Their sin has meant riches (an eternal inheritance) for the Gentiles
- Their return will bring even greater riches

Even some of the great evangelicals have dismissed the Jews as an irrelevance—a nation with a past but no future.

Paul rejects the idea that their fall should even be considered as beyond recovery. On the contrary, he sees their restoration as bringing riches; the theme of abundance that we saw again and again in Old Testament prophecy. Not only that, but their stumbling has allowed salvation to come to the Gentiles, as Simeon's prayer in the temple testified.

What is more, Paul addresses these remarks squarely to the Gentiles. Now if all scripture is inspired of God (which it is) then shouldn't we sit up and take note when we are told we are being addressed! It is no coincidence that Paul wrote this message all those years ago, so it might be here for us to see and understand in our age. The same theme is continued in Romans eleven, where he writes; *'For if their rejection is the reconciliation of the world, what will their acceptance be but life from the dead?'*[9]

I cannot help but be drawn back to Ezekiel and the valley of

---

8   Romans 11:11-12
9   Romans 11:15

dry bones. When God showed him the vast army as bleached bones, Ezekiel knew that God alone was able to make life come from death. I wonder if that passage was in Paul's mind as he spoke of their acceptance as being *'life from the dead'?*

Paul goes on to liken Israel to an olive tree. Some of the branches, he admits, have been broken off and Gentile believers have been grafted in. It is yet another reminder that we are to be a part of the commonwealth of Israel, sharing in the eternal promises of God, available to all who believe in Jesus. But with the promise of our ingrafting comes a warning: *do not boast over those branches . . . Do not be arrogant, but be afraid. For if God did not spare the natural branches, he will not spare you either.*[10]

Paul could hardly be clearer. Wherever you think you stand, don't consider yourselves better or somehow more worthy than the Jews. Sadly, through many centuries, the Christian church seems to have missed this warning. Even some of the great evangelicals have dismissed the Jews as an irrelevance —a nation with a past but no future. How wrong can we be! We need to line ourselves up with God's promises, not look to put them aside. It is time for the church to wake up.

Now we have been grafted in, from foreign root stock as it were, but Paul explains that the Jews (those cut off) can be rejoined by skilful husbandry: *How much more readily will these, the natural branches, be grafted into their own olive tree!*[11]

Paul now leads us to the climax of this whole matter of Israel. *I do not want you to be ignorant of this mystery, brothers, so that you may not be conceited: Israel has experienced a hardening in part until the full number of the Gentiles has come in. And so all Israel will be saved, as it is written: "The deliverer will come from Zion; He will turn godlessness away from Jacob. And this is My covenant with them when I take away their sins." As far as the gospel is concerned they are*

10   Romans 11:20
11   Romans 11:24

enemies on your account; but as far as election is concerned, they are loved on account of the patriarchs, for God's gifts and His call are irrevocable.[12]

Let's be certain of what Paul is saying:

- Believers, don't be ignorant about God's plans
- Ignorance leads to a false conceit
- The hearts of Israel have been hardened in part until all the Gentiles who are called have come to God
- All Israel will be saved
- God Himself will turn away godlessness from Jacob
- That is God's personal covenant with them when He takes away their sins
- As far as the gospel is concerned they are enemies
- As far as election (or calling) is concerned they are loved
- God's gift and calling are irrevocable

Now I have heard theologians determinedly state that we are the Israel of God and that Israel as a nation is merely an accident of modern history. This passage and our study of scripture so far, prove them conclusively wrong, but let's deal with their objections, by agreeing for a moment they are correct, and substituting their language for Paul's language in this passage.

One of the prime arguments of these theologians is that where Israel is mentioned in the New Testament it should be understood as the Church, but in this passage not only do we find reference to Israel but also to Jacob. Are we really to believe this applies to the church? Let's humour this party and try a little experiment, substituting the word Church for the word Israel. Romans eleven, verse twelve now reads: 'salvation has come to the Gentiles to make the Church envious.' It makes nonsense of scripture! In fact, on almost

12   Romans 11:25-29

every occasion (over sixty times) the word Israel is used in the New Testament, the context is the nation and people generically known as the Jews.

Paul, writing by the Holy Spirit, points out that these promises have everything to do with God's eternal covenants, and nothing to do with our own good works. No wonder he is caught up in praise of God when he realises just what is going to happen:

O the depth of the riches of the wisdom and knowledge of God!

How unsearchable His judgements,

And His paths beyond tracing out!

"Who has known the mind of the Lord?

Or who has been His counsellor?

Who has ever given to God,

That God should repay him?"

For from Him and through Him and to Him are all things.

To Him be the glory for ever! Amen.[13]

Paul's message is entirely consistent with the message and thrust of all the Old Testament prophets—punishment, scattering and finally deliverance; never again to be taken from the land. Once more we are faced with the realization that short of gross distortion we cannot escape the continuing themes of God's love and God's eternal covenants with Israel.

---

13   Romans 11:33-36

Chapter 16

CORINTHIANS: THE WISDOM OF GOD IN SALVATION

But thanks be to God, who always leads us in triumphal procession in Christ and through us spreads everywhere the fragrance of the knowledge of Him.

2 Corinthians 2:14

Our final scripture from Romans saw Paul, caught up in praise and wonder at God's amazing plans, which he described as *unsearchable* and *beyond tracing out.*[1] Hidden away in Paul's letter to the Corinthians, letters to a vibrant but ill-disciplined Church, we find further confirmation that God's plans for His people are indeed beyond our understanding

---

The death and resurrection of Jesus are humanly illogical.

Paul, an outstandingly gifted man in the natural sense, wished to make clear to the disparate group of believers in the Corinthian Church that they were in danger of being sidetracked by their fascination with intellectual prowess. The gospel has never been dependent on intellect.

1   Romans 11:33

For the message of the cross is foolishness to those who are perishing, but to us who are being saved it is the power of God. For it is written: "I will destroy the wisdom of the wise; the intelligence of the intelligent I will frustrate." Where is the wise man? Where is the scholar? Where is the philosopher of this age? Has not God made foolish the wisdom of the world? For since in the wisdom of God the world through its wisdom did not know Him, God was pleased through the foolishness of what was preached to save those who believe. Jews demand miraculous signs and Greeks look for wisdom, but we preach Christ crucified: a stumbling block to Jews and foolishness to Gentiles, but to those whom God has called, both Jews and Greeks, Christ the power of God and the wisdom of God.[2]

Paul says that in one sense God has turned human reasoning on its head:

- The death and resurrection of Jesus are humanly illogical
- The Jewish nation were looking for a Messiah who would save them from the Romans, not one who would allow Himself to be crucified
- The Jewish nation were looking for a Messiah who would demonstrate His power by the miraculous
- Christ's crucifixion was alien to their concept of a Messiah, for scripture taught them that *anyone who is hung on a tree is under God's curse*[3]
- But to those Jews called, Christ was the power of God and the wisdom of God

This, in a nutshell, is the dilemma for the Jew to this day. It is a dilemma amplified by the blood sacrifice of Jesus and the symbolism of the breaking of bread. *The Lord Jesus, on the night He was betrayed, took bread, and when He had given thanks, He broke it and said, "This is My body, which is for*

2   1 Corinthians 1:18-24
3   Deuteronomy 21:23

you; do this in remembrance of Me." In the same way, after supper He took the cup, saying, "This cup is the new covenant in My blood; do this, whenever you drink it, in remembrance of Me." For whenever you eat this bread and drink this cup, you proclaim the Lord's death until He comes.[4]

The Jewish nation were looking for a Messiah who would save them from the Romans, not one who would allow Himself to be crucified.

This blood sacrifice stands in direct opposition to the arguments of those who say that a third temple is needed, with its continual need for sacrifice. Does this blood sacrifice of Christ then mean that the vast majority of Jews will find themselves excluded? The second epistle to the Corinthians suggests otherwise: *For no matter how many promises God has made, they are "Yes" in Christ. And so through Him the "Amen" is spoken by us to the glory of God.*[5] For the Gentile believer, there is a present and real hope; for the Jew, shut up in 'stupor' until the fullness of the Gentiles has come in, there is both future promise and future hope.

The epistles to the Corinthian Church point us one further time to God's unfailing love and to his grace for all mankind, Jew and Gentile alike.

---

4   1 Corinthians 11:23-26
5.   2 Corinthians 1:20

Chapter 17

GALATIANS: GOOD NEWS FOR JEW AND GENTILE

From the letters to the Corinthians, with their challenge to both Jew and Gentile to live in Godly freedom under the Lordship of Jesus, we turn to Galatians. The battle lines have been drawn early on in the history of the Church: battle lines that still exist in today's 21st century Church. To some in Galatia there was an insistence on regulations and procedure in order to bring believers to a place where they stood, fully immersed (as these teachers saw it) in the traditions of the Old Testament.

Paul does not waste time on his introduction, nor does he try to hide his deep concerns over their behaviour. He tells them bluntly, *I am astonished you are so quickly deserting the One who called you by grace of Christ and are turning to a different gospel . . . But even if we or an angel from heaven should preach a gospel other than the one we preached to you, let him be eternally condemned! As we have already said, so now I say again: If anybody is preaching to you a gospel other than what you accepted, let him be eternally condemned!*[1]

What is it that so upsets him so much? It is the replacement of the full gospel about Jesus with a system devised by man. But he wants the Church to be in no doubt that the gospel is *not something that man made up.*[2] Paul can see the tendency of the early Church (as the Church has done ever since), to embrace dead aspects of Jewish law. Even dear Peter does not

1   Galatians 1:6, 8-9 extracted
2   Galatians 1:11

escape Paul's censure and indeed is used as an example.

Peter had been eating with the Gentiles, something which under the old covenant the Jews had been taught not to do, but which was cancelled under his new freedom in Jesus. When men arrived who were associated with James, Peter *began to draw back and separate himself . . . other Jews joined him in his hypocrisy, so that . . . even Barnabas was led astray.*[3] Paul was having none of it and challenged Peter to his face. *"You are a Jew, yet you live like a Gentile and not like a Jew. How is it, then, that you force Gentiles to follow Jewish customs? We who are Jews by birth and not 'Gentile sinners' know that a man is not justified by observing the law, but by faith in Jesus Christ. So we too, have put our faith in Christ Jesus that we might be justified by faith and not by observing the law, because by observing the law no-one will be justified . . . for if righteousness could be gained through the law, Christ died for nothing!"*[4]

The message in this passage is still a stumbling block today, to Jew and Gentile alike. There are calls to go back to Celtic roots, calls to go back to Wesleyan roots and calls to look towards Jewish observance. Paul is absolute in condemnation of such 'religious' forms of worship. There are still those who would trap us under law, but God has set us free from that.

As far as Paul was concerned, the Galatians had been *bewitched . . . Did you receive the Spirit by observing the law, or by believing what you heard? . . . are you now trying to attain your goal by human effort? . . . All who rely on observing the law are under a curse . . . Christ redeemed us from the curse of the law by becoming a curse for us . . .*[5] Further on in the chapter we find Paul explaining why the law was necessary: *The law was put in charge to lead us to Christ that we might be justified by faith. Now that faith has come, we are no longer under the supervision of the law.*[6]

Paul is not yet finished with this very real danger to a living

3   Galatians 2:12-13 extracted
4   Galatians 2:14-16 and 21
5   Galatians 3:1,2,3, 10 and 13 extracted
6   Galatians 3:24-25

church. In chapter four he continues his theme: *How is it that you are turning back to those weak and miserable principles? Do you wish to be enslaved by them all over again? You are observing special days and months and seasons and years! I fear for you, that somehow I have wasted my efforts on you.*[7] While we may learn valuable insights from Jewish customs, we must resist absolutely any attempt to place us under the yoke of practices that were completed in and through the risen work of the Messiah, Jesus Christ.

> . . . grace reaches far beyond the
> logic of the human heart . . .

There is one more area we should mention before we leave this epistle, a chestnut of ancient origin but inevitably widely quoted out of context when it comes to establishing God's promises to Israel: *There is neither Jew nor Greek, slave nor free, male or female, for you are all one in Christ Jesus. If you belong to Christ, then you are Abraham's seed, and heirs according to the promise.*[8] The major theme of this epistle, as we have already seen, is freedom from the law and this passage fits firmly into that context. You cannot make demands under the law because of a person's race or sex.

It begins with a statement that we are all sons of God through faith in Christ Jesus. That is true, but to take that statement out of context and argue that it proves men and women have equal function and that Jew and Gentile are irrelevant, is to miss the context both of Galatians as an epistle and Paul's teaching throughout the New Testament. Paul has already explained how he and Peter had different callings: *For God, who was at work in the ministry of Peter as an apostle to the Jews, was also at work in my ministry as an apostle to the Gentiles . . . they agreed that we should go to the Gentiles,*

7 Galatians 4:9-11
8 Galatians 3:28-29

and they to the Jews.[9] God had clear ministries to reach different groups. Paul and those with him, had their greatest success among Gentiles; Peter, James and John among those of Jewish descent.

Paul's teaching, as we have already seen from Romans, recognises God's plans for Israel as a nation and their specific role in God's end-time purposes. We are, indeed, heirs of the promise. It is unfortunate that many modern translations render Ephesians two verse twelve as *citizenship in Israel* when the more accurate translation is that of the King James, which refers to us as *members of the commonwealth of Israel.* All those who know Jesus as Lord have an eternal inheritance and are loved of the Lord, but we have different roles to play in bringing God's kingdom to pass.

But above all, this epistle shows us that grace reaches far beyond the logic of the human heart and brings us to a place where we may see our petty rules and regulations for what they really are—hindrances to the promises that are there, for Jew and Gentile alike, in the gift of the Messiah, the Lord Jesus.

9   Galatians 2:8-9

Chapter 18

HEBREWS: JESUS OUR GREAT HIGH PRIEST

Therefore, brothers, since we have confidence to enter the most Holy Place by the blood of Jesus, by a new and living way opened for us through the curtain, that is, His body, and since we have a great priest over the house of God, let us draw near to God with a sincere heart in full assurance of faith . . .

Hebrews 10:19-22

From the book of Galatians, with its impassioned plea for freedom in Christ, we turn to Hebrews. Many Jewish believers were finding themselves under attack for their new-found faith in Christ. Paul urges them not to be tempted to return to the safe haven of what they already knew. He happily accepted that the law and the prophets would inform their understanding, but these were but a pale shadow of what was to be found in the Messiah, Jesus.

In outlining his opening argument, he talks of Moses as *faithful in all God's house* but of Jesus being *found worthy of greater honour than Moses, just as the builder of a house has greater honour than the house itself.*[1] Why then is this?

To Paul, the essence of it is in the office that Jesus holds. Under Jewish law, as laid out through Moses, it was the great high priest who came once a year into the holiest of holies, to offer a sacrifice for the sin of the people. *Every high priest is*

---

1 Hebrews 3:2-3

selected from among men and is appointed to represent them in matters related to God, to offer gifts and sacrifices for sins. He is able to deal gently with those who are ignorant and are going astray, since he himself is subject to weakness. This is why he has to offer sacrifices for his own sins, as well as for the sins of the people.[2]

As Aaron, the original high priest of the Old Testament was called, so too was Jesus. *Christ also did not take upon Himself the glory of becoming a high priest. But God said to Him, "You are My Son; today I have become Your Father" . . . He learned obedience from what He suffered and, once made perfect, He became the source of eternal salvation for all who obey Him and was designated by God to be high priest in the order of Melchizedek.*[3]

So for everyone God has called, both Jew and Gentile, Jesus has become both Messiah and high priest in the order of Melchizedek and as such, our high priest forever.

God Himself is committed to this covenant; therefore we can see that it becomes, like the covenants God swore to the patriarchs, something that is unalterable. *Because of this oath, Jesus has become the guarantee of a better covenant.*[4]

Paul is at pains to reinforce both the timeless nature and absolute certainty of this new covenant, a covenant that shows the law to be but a shadow of what God had intended for man, from the time God first began to work out His plan of salvation for all mankind. How are we all, Jew and Gentile alike, to understand this high priest?

Paul describes him as:

- *Holy*
- *Blameless*
- *Set apart from sinners*
- *Exalted above the heavens*

2 Hebrews 5:1-3
3 Hebrews 5:5-10 extracted
4 Hebrews 7:22

- *Sacrificed for their sins once for all*
- *Made perfect for ever*
- *Seated at the right hand of God*
- *Serving in the sanctuary of the true tabernacle set up by the Lord, not man[5]*

So for everyone God has called, both Jew and Gentile, Jesus has become both Messiah and high priest in the order of Melchizedek and as such, our high priest forever.

For Israel the significance of this description is in its divine scope. Paul identifies Jeremiah's prophetic message with the advent of the new covenant, which is theirs in Christ Jesus. God *"will make a new covenant with the house of Israel and the House of Judah . . . This is the covenant I will make with the House of Israel after that time, declares the Lord. I will put My laws in their minds and write them on their hearts. I will be their God, and they will be My people . . . I will forgive their wickedness and remember their sins no more."[6]* For Paul, Christ's death and resurrection brought Israel closer to the full and total restoration they could never have achieved under the law. It did not separate them from God but made them candidates for undeserved mercy and grace.

This is so as, *The law is only a shadow of the good things that are coming[7]* The high priest was condemned to offer the same *religious duties* day after day, whereas Christ, when He had *offered for all time the one sacrifice for sins . . . sat down at the right hand of God.[8]* What is Paul's conclusion of the state of the Jewish people at this time? It is simple. When God has

---

5   Hebrews 7:26 to 8:2
6   Hebrews 8:8-12 quoting Jeremiah 31
7   Hebrews 10:1
8   Hebrews 10:12

wiped away their sins and lawless acts, *there is no longer any sacrifice for sin.*[9]

For Gentile and Jew alike, this takes place, or will take place, through faith in Jesus as King and High Priest. *Now faith is being sure of what we hope for and certain of what we do not see.*[10] When Paul sets out to give practical illustrations of faith, it is to the Jewish nation and to the Jews of previous generations that he turns. Far from being abandoned by God, these men, from God's chosen people, serve as examples to us all. This *great cloud of witnesses*[11] are Jewish, and are an example to the whole Church of God's response to man's faith.

What then, is Paul's ultimate conclusion? Simply this: *Therefore, since we are receiving a kingdom that cannot be shaken, let us be thankful, and so worship God acceptably with reverence and awe, for our "God is a consuming fire."*[12]

For us, as Gentile Christians, Hebrews becomes a certain anchor for our own faith. For the Jewish nation, it further reinforces the love of God for his people; a love as deeply imbedded throughout the New Testament as the Old.

9　Hebrews 10:18
10　Hebrews 11:1
11　Hebrews 12:1
12　Hebrews 12:28-29

Chapter 19

REVELATION: ISRAEL'S FUTURE HOPE

"Now the dwelling of God is with men, and He will live with them. They will be His people, and God Himself will be with them and be their God."

Revelation 21:3

I want to tread carefully through the book of Revelation. Much of the theme of John's great prophecy is set in the end times, much is still to come, but it is God's Word and it shows us, yet again, the nation of Israel in a central position as this age draws to a close.

At Jesus' ascension, two angels asked the disciples, *"Men of Galilee . . . why do you stand here looking into the sky? This same Jesus, who has been taken from you into heaven, will come back in the same way you have seen Him go into heaven."*[1] We can be certain from this statement that Israel's Messiah, the Lord Jesus Christ, will return to the same place and in the same manner as He ascended. Jesus, the King of the Jews, will come back to Jerusalem.

I am a literalist, as regards what the Bible says, which is probably an unwise statement to make as we come to the book of Revelation! Unless the Bible speaks of something as being figurative or symbolic, or defines it as such by context, I expect prophecy to unfold as it is predicted. Where language is figurative, it is normally obvious. When the Bible

1 Acts 1:11

refers to *"the Lion of the tribe of Judah, the Root of David,"*[2] it is plainly referring to Jesus as King of the Jews. That said, can we find supporting evidence for the return of Jesus, the Jewish Messiah, in this last book of the New Testament?

In the opening chapter of Revelation Jesus is referred to as:

- *The faithful witness*
- *The firstborn from the dead*
- *The ruler of the kings of the earth*[3]

The passage continues: *Look, He is coming with the clouds, and every eye will see Him, even those who pierced Him; and all the peoples of the earth will mourn because of Him. So shall it be! Amen. "I am the Alpha and the Omega," says the Lord God, "who is, and who was, and who is to come, the Almighty."*[4]

This is the majestic, risen Christ, of awesome power and appearance. John was so overwhelmed that he fell at his feet, but Jesus encouraged him with these words: *"Do not be afraid. I am the First and the Last. I am the Living One; I was dead, and behold I am alive for ever and ever! And I hold the keys of Death and Hades."*[5]

This Jewish Messiah is:

- The first and the Last
- The Living One
- The One who holds the keys of Death and Hades

He is hailed by the angels and by every creature on earth and under the earth. *Then I looked and heard the voice of many angels, numbering thousands upon thousands, and ten thousand times ten thousand . . . In a loud voice they sang: "Worthy is the Lamb, who was slain, to receive power and wealth and wisdom and strength and honour and glory and praise!" Then I heard every creature in heaven and on earth and under the earth and on the sea, and all that is in them,*

2   Revelation 5:5
3   Revelation 1:5
4   Revelation 1:7-8
5   Revelation 1:18

*singing: "To Him who sits on the throne and to the Lamb be
praise and honour and glory and power, for ever and ever!"
The four living creatures said, "Amen," and the elders fell
down and worshipped.*[6]

But if there is a triumphant, risen Christ at the centre of the
world's stage at this time, is there a place for His ancient
people, Israel?

In this last great book of the Bible, part of the final purpose
of God concerns the sealing of *144,000 from all the tribes of
Israel.*[7] An exact and equable distribution is carried out
between the tribes. This refers specifically to the children of
Israel. Nowhere in the New Testament are Gentile Christians
delineated as members of Judah, Reuben, Gad, etc. So here
once more, in Revelation, far from being cast off, the children
of Israel play a central role.

It is almost as if we can hear
Jesus, the Messiah, the Son of
God of endless compassion,
reaching down through the
centuries and saying; "And tell
My people I am still their
Messiah. Tell them I still love
them and tell them they have a
certain future."

One major problem in understanding scripture is our own
pride: none of us are immune to it. When we read prophecy
we want to be the ones in the position of importance.
Accepting our calling and our rightful place in God's plans
will bring us our full reward. God wants us to use our talents,

6   Revelation 5:11-14
7   Revelation 7:4

but He doesn't want us to try and steal those belonging to other people. We have seen our inclusion and our inheritance categorically promised, so we don't need to be envious of someone else's. God will use Jewish people in very specific way in the end-times—let's be glad about it, not jealous. If we take the trouble to read on to the following verse, we should forget any such jealousy, for here is the guarantee of our own salvation.

After this I looked and there before me was a great multitude that no-one could count, from every nation, tribe, people and language, standing before the throne and in front of the Lamb. They were wearing white robes and were holding palm branches in their hands. And they cried out in a loud voice: "Salvation belongs to our God, who sits on the throne, and to the Lamb."[8]

What had been implicit in the Old Testament, and had been made explicit in the New Testament through the teaching of Paul, is confirmed and sealed at the end of the age. The Jewish Messiah brings salvation for Gentile believers *from every nation, tribe, people and language.*

Following the judgements of chapters eight to thirteen, we find what we must assume are these same 144,000 from the tribes of Israel, with the Lamb (Jesus) at the start of chapter fourteen. *Then I looked, and there before me was the Lamb, standing on Mount Zion, and with Him 144,000 who had His name and His Father's name written on their foreheads . . . They were purchased from among men and offered as firstfruits to God and the Lamb. No lie was found in their mouths; they are blameless.*[9] I am not asking you to build a theology on this, but to me it is a wonderful reminder of the early disciples, who left everything to follow Jesus. Only here, just in case anyone is wondering about a Judas, their heart attitude is stated: *'No lie was found in their mouths; they are blameless.'*

From this passage we pass on to the final stages of God's

8   Revelation 7:9-10
9   Revelation 14:1-5 extracted

re-creation: *Then I saw a new heaven and a new earth, for the first heaven and the first earth had passed away, and there was no longer any sea. I saw the Holy City, the New Jerusalem, coming down out of heaven from God, prepared as a bride beautifully dressed for her husband. And I heard a loud voice from the throne saying, "Now the dwelling of God is with men, and He will live with them. They will be His people, and God Himself will be with them and be their God. He will wipe every tear from their eyes. There will be no more death or mourning or crying or pain, for the old order of things has passed away."*[10]

What a wonderful picture; what a vision of the future. As we look back through the centuries of persecution, we see a new hope for the Jews and the Jewish nation. No more pogroms, no more fears of a second holocaust. And for ourselves, called into this commonwealth of Israel, *"no more death or mourning or crying or pain."*

Later, in this same chapter, we read of the New Jerusalem: *'On the gates were written the names of the twelve tribes of Israel . . . The wall of the city had twelve foundations and on them were the names of the twelve apostles of the Lamb.'*[11] For those who believe the Church has replaced Israel we have yet another problem—The gates have the names of tribes upon them and the Jewish apostles are part of the foundation of the New Jerusalem.

In the gospel accounts we read how Peter, who had sworn he would never betray Jesus, had three times vehemently denied he knew him. After Jesus' resurrection, when the women discover Jesus has risen, an angel instructs them: *"Tell His disciples and tell Peter."*[12]

When we read these verses it is almost as if we can hear Jesus, the Messiah, the Son of the God of endless compassion, reaching down through the centuries and saying, "And tell My people I am still their Messiah. Tell them I still love them and

10 Revelation 21:1-4
11 Revelation 21:12
12 Mark 16:7

tell them they have a certain future."

Revelation twenty-two concludes the triumphant work of God through Jesus: *"I, Jesus, have sent My angel to you to give you this testimony for the churches. I am the Root and Offspring of David, and the bright Morning Star."*[13] Jesus wants Jew and Gentile to be sure of this testimony, and certain that these events will all come to pass.

The message is for the churches, but once more Jesus is *"the Root and Offspring of David."* Again, through this title, the Messiah offers a future hope and a future kingdom to the nation God chose for himself; Israel and the Jewish nation.

Therefore, with a total conviction and certainty we can join with the Spirit and the Bride and say: *"Come!" And let him who hears say, "Come!" Whoever is thirsty, let him come; and whoever wishes, let him take the free gift of the water of life.*[14]

The testimony of God's Word, from Genesis to Revelation, is grace. The testimony of God, from Abraham to John, is faithfulness. God is a covenant-keeping God and His plans for His people are unshakeable. As we see what He does for and through His people Israel, may we pray for them as we see God preparing them and us, together, for the return of the Lord Jesus Christ in power and glory.

---

13   Revelation 22:16
14   Revelation 22:17

CHAPTER 20

HISTORICAL BACKGROUND PART ONE: FROM THE ROMANS TO HITLER

"O Jerusalem, Jerusalem, you who kill the prophets and stone those sent to you, how often have I longed to gather your children together, as a hen gathers her chicks under her wings, but you were not willing."

Matthew 23:37

The purpose of this book has been to present a biblical perspective of the past, present and future place of the Jewish nation. For this reason, I want to resist the very strong temptation to give a detailed history of the land and the people of Israel from the birth of Jesus to the present day. However, to inform our understanding, an outline of the last 2,000 years is helpful. Where I have thought a date or map sufficient, I have left it at that. Elsewhere, additional comments are added to provide explanation. As far as possible I have attempted to ensure historical accuracy, though there may be disagreements about exact timescales.

Today, Hollywood has a fascination with violence and destruction on an epic scale. The Jewish people have lived through violence and destruction for the last 2,000 years. The avowed intent of many extremists today is the total destruction of a Jewish State that is, to them, anathema—but we will return to that later. The first of the historical events we consider is the destruction of Jerusalem, which took place in AD 70.

Jesus had warned of the devastation of Jerusalem and the temple, when he spoke to some of the disciples about the signs of the end of the age. They had been remarking on the building's beauty, something which was no doubt true. Even though it could not be compared to Solomon's temple, it was a wonderful work of art. But Jesus said: *"As for what you see here, the time will come when not one stone will be left on another; every one of them will be thrown down."*[1] He continued later in His discourse: *"When you see Jerusalem surrounded by armies, you will know that its desolation is near. Then let those who are in Judea flee to the mountains, let those in the city get out, and let those in the country not enter the city. For this is the time of punishment in fulfilment of all that has been written. How dreadful it will be in those days for pregnant women and nursing mothers! There will be great distress in the land and wrath against this people. They will fall by the sword and will be taken as prisoners to all the nations. Jerusalem will be trampled on by the Gentiles until the times of the Gentiles are fulfilled."*[2]

Luke nineteen paints an even clearer description of how this would take place. *He (Jesus) approached Jerusalem and saw the city, He wept over it and said, "If you, even you, had only known on this day what would bring your peace—but now it is hidden from your eyes. The days will come upon you when your enemies will build an embankment against you and encircle you and hem you in on every side. They will dash you to the ground, you and the children within your walls. They will not leave one stone upon another, because you did not recognise the time of God's coming upon you."*[3]

1   Luke 21:6
2   Luke 21:20-24
3   Luke 19:41-44

Tragically, like many of Jesus' previous calls to follow Him, these words remained unheeded by the vast majority of the Jewish people. As we have mentioned elsewhere, there is evidence that when these events were unfolding the early church recognised the warning signs and fled the country. However, for those who didn't have ears to hear, the situation could have hardly have been more different.

Historians tell us that Jerusalem was crowded to capacity when the final siege began. It was the time of Passover and more than half a million extra visitors were there. According to records, there were three vast walls that protected Jerusalem, but over a period of months each successive wall was destroyed. Those who tried to flee were caught and crucified, until we are told there were no more trees with which to make crosses. Eventually the city was taken. The temple was set ablaze and those who were left were either slaughtered or taken into captivity and dispersed as slaves around the Roman Empire. Estimates put the number of Jews who died in the siege as high as one million.

It was the forerunner of an ethnic Jewish holocaust that would be mirrored in the twentieth century, by a man who modelled much of what he did on the Roman system he so admired. The man was Adolph Hitler and the country was Nazi Germany— but there was to be much more suffering for the Jews of the dispersion before that horrific nightmare in the history of Israel.

Some time between AD 130 and 135 a false messiah, Bar Kochba, managed to persuade sufficient Jews that he was the liberator they had been waiting for. He and his followers revolted against Roman rule. The rebellion's final act was the mass suicide at Masada, which had held out for over three years against Roman siege. Over the period of the rebellion thousands more Jews had been slaughtered. More significantly for the land of Israel, this rebellion was the last straw for the Romans in their dealing with the Jews.

They set out to eradicate any names or symbols that might be used as a rallying point by these wretched Jews. The Romans banished all but a very few of the poorest Jews from the country. They changed the name of the country to Palestine (the land of the Philistines). It is the name commonly used nowadays and in the late eighties, some Palestinian youths were happy to claim to be Philistines, the ancient enemies of Israel. Interestingly, the Romans also changed the name of Jerusalem to Aelia Capitolina, but this name change did not last.

At the same time as these tragic events had been unfolding, Jewish communities elsewhere had determinedly continued to hand down their verbal versions of Jewish law. These had started with the oral law of the scribes, who had then moved to the Midrash, the exposition of scripture. From that came the Mishna, influenced by Greek teaching, although all of these referred to the Bible as the basic text. Jesus however, did not approve of this additional codification. In Luke he says to them: *"Woe to you experts in the law, because you have taken away the key of knowledge. You yourselves have not entered, and you have hindered those who were entering."*[4]

As we arrive at the third century AD, we find the teaching of the Mishna closed and the Gemara, or supplement, begun. Significantly, this moved things a step further away from scripture by regarding the Mishna as the text for exposition. By the time of the Talmud, the written version of the Mishna and the Gemara, begun in the fourth century and then written in the last years of the fifth century, these exegeses had grown to some 2,500,000 words. A new Dark Age, which was to mirror that of Europe, had begun for the Jewish people.

Meanwhile, for the early Church, persecution had continued. Its most famous writer, Paul, had been martyred in Rome, probably about AD 68. Roman emperors, most notable

4 Luke 11:52

among whom was Nero, sought to use Christians as an excuse for internal troubles; blaming them for much that went wrong. They killed, tortured and abused them as live entertainment in their barbaric coliseums.

By the start of the fourth century the Roman Empire was administratively divided. The emperor Diocletian hounded the Christians, but this was to be the last great persecution of the early Church. In 313 AD Constantine became Roman Emperor and declared Christianity to be a good religion and one which he purportedly adopted himself, though historians are divided as to whether his conversion was genuine or a matter of expedience.

From that time on the Christian Church enjoyed a time of peace and growth, but for the Jews it heralded a time of renewed persecution, which has continued to the present day.

Some historians have reported that one of Constantine's first acts after his conversion was to outlaw the Jews. The Emperor Justinian, in the first part of the sixth century, followed in these footsteps. He abolished their synagogues, refused them citizenship and appropriated property, saying they didn't have the right to pass it to anyone else, including their natural heirs.

As for the remnants of Israel, wherever they fled, the Jews found further persecution. Certainly they were tolerated and, in some cases, even encouraged for a period of years in Europe. They were good moneylenders and providers of finance. This was a job which was beneath the dignity of the landed nobility or the guilds of the day (from which Jews were often excluded). It was however, a necessary part of life, much as it is today, and Jews were permitted to undertake it. Latent anti-Semitism though, was never far beneath the surface.

The Crusades, ostensibly to free the 'Holy Land', became an

excuse for appalling acts of savagery against the Jewish population. In 1096 an estimated 10,000 Jews were slaughtered in the Rhineland, by Crusaders on their way to Jerusalem. Once there, they massacred most of the Moslems and the Jews, torching synagogues and burning to death the people who had fled there to take refuge.

One by-product of the above carnage was that Jerusalem's population fell to its lowest recorded level, some 3,000. It remained a poor and neglected community until the latter part of the nineteenth century.

As already stated, it is not the intention to detail the full list of calumnies against the Jews, but to give illustrative examples of their suffering. England expelled all Jews for a period of 400 years. In parts of the country, pogroms were carried out and whole Jewish communities were massacred or burnt alive. The same was true all over Europe.

In the aftermath of the Black Death, which was estimated to have killed up to three-quarters of the population of Europe, Jews found themselves blamed yet again. In Switzerland Jews were burned alive on the shores of Lake Geneva, while in Strasbourg in the following year, 1349, a Jewish community of almost 2,000 were thrown alive onto an enormous fire.

Under the Spanish inquisition Jews suffered some of the worst persecution since the Roman Empire, before Spain banished the remaining Jews from their shores. On the day that Columbus set out on the voyage of discovery that led him to America, a great exodus of Jews were in the process of boarding ships that would take them to new lands.

Prior to the twentieth century, probably the worst excesses took place in Russia. In 1881 the Russian Orthodox Church issued a proclamation, which said that one third of the Jews in the country should be forcibly converted to the Russian

Church, one third should be expelled from the country and one third should be exterminated. We can make no excuse for these church leaders, but they would not have succeeded without the support of the Czars. Indeed, it is more than probable that the churches' edict was issued to curry favour with the anti-Semitic rulers of the time.

Czar Nicholas I had forbidden Jews to move outside an area known as the 'Pale of Settlement.' Alexander III had continued and expanded upon that policy. There is no doubt that with the enormous influence it wielded over the people, the Orthodox Church made it much easier for Nicholas II to carry out the murderous and extensive pogroms of the early part of the twentieth century. In the light of such facts it comes as no surprise that the Russian royal family was totally wiped out in the revolution that followed. God is never indifferent to the suffering of His people.

However, the spread of Communism did not bring the relief which might have been hoped. 1,500,000 people were forcibly moved to the interior at twelve hours notice. Across Russia, somewhere between 500,000 to 1,000,000 Jews were killed. The systematic slaughter, rape and torture of Jews became commonplace. The Russian authorities took little pains to hide their deeds from the world. People might still talk about these atrocities today, were it not that an even more violent and destructive Satanic force was being prepared against them. It found its vent in Nazi Germany.

The rise of Hitler and the Nazi party in 1930s' Germany is well documented. From September 1935 openly anti-Semitic laws were passed, but a campaign of anti-Semitism had been operating long before that. Bismarck had used it in the nineteenth century to discredit the Jews and mutterings had long been going in German society about the undue prominence and wealth of the Jewish population. They were, so the rumours went, secretly planning to take over the State.

Discrimination became the order of the day.

Jews found themselves openly blamed for whatever the speaker chose to include at public rallies. Members of the Nazi party began to daub Jewish property with slogans; Jews were beaten up and their homes invaded. Those who could understand what was taking place began to leave Germany, but many were too slow to see what was happening and besides, Hitler had plans that extended beyond Germany, to regions where the Jewish population thought themselves safe.

The next stage had a tragic inevitability, given all that had gone before. Jewish property was seized; Jews were forbidden by edict to own businesses or to practise a profession. Month by month the pressure increased, but it was nothing compared to that which the Nazis planned—the wholesale destruction of the Jewish people.

Despite the denial of those on the extreme right of European politics, who insist that the holocaust never took place, the Second World War saw the largest systematic destruction of an ethnic group ever undertaken. At the start of the Second World War, Hitler, at one of his vast and widely reported rallies, told his audience: "It will bring forth the final annihilation of the Jewish nation in Europe." For Germans to say they knew nothing of Hitler's plans begs the question of whether they attended rallies, listened to the radio or read the newspapers where his speeches were widely reported. However, there is no doubt that the allies were also aware of what was going on.

Over 6,000,000 Jews (along with many gypsies, Poles and other groups) were exterminated in the concentration camps. They were treated with utter inhumanity. Herded onto cattle trucks they were systematically eliminated from vast regions of Europe. Those who dared to protest or offer shelter to Jews were themselves at risk of being shot. Himmler, the chief of the SS, said of the so-called 'final solution': "We have undertaken an important and difficult task with great skill and with no harm to ourselves or to our consciences." (My paraphrase.)

At the start of the Second World War, Hitler, at one of his vast and widely reported rallies, told his audience: "It will bring forth the final annihilation of the Jewish nation in Europe."

By the time Germany surrendered in 1945, the Jewish population across Europe had been decimated. A horrified world began to see for themselves the full extent of the demonic campaign waged by Hitler and his followers against the Jews, God's chosen nation. It was, sadly, a lesson of which the British took little cognisance in the years that followed; but in the first part of the twentieth century, much had been going on that made the creation of the State of Israel a possibility.

For centuries Jews of the Diaspora had spoken wistfully of returning to Jerusalem, of re-creating a Jewish State, but despite well-meaning rhetoric and a trickle of returnees, it seemed to most Jews a distant dream; however, a stirring in the heart of world Jewry changed all that.

1897 saw the first World Zionist Congress in Basle, Switzerland. There Theodore Herzl, considered by many to be the founding light of the modern Jewish State, spoke of his vision of a recreated Israel. He admitted it might seem like a foolish dream but, he assured his audience, within fifty years it would be a reality. Although Herzl would not live to see it (He died in 1904, aged forty-four), he had been instrumental in driving forward a movement of Jews around the world who, disparate in background, had one common aim, the creation of a modern Jewish State.

At the same time, there were many, Christian and non-Christian, who were sympathetic to a national homeland for the Jews. Through the tireless lobbying of Chaim Weizmann and others, Britain was stirred to respond to this growing Jewish desire for their own land. The Balfour declaration of 1917 stated: "His Majesty's Government views with favour the establishment in Palestine of a national home for the Jewish people, and will use its best endeavours to facilitate the achievement of this object . . . "

Jews had already been returning to Israel in increasing numbers during the latter part of the nineteenth century. Balfour's declaration did not, of itself, cause a great influx of migrants, but it did encourage those already there and provided the prospect of a safe haven for many who felt embattled in the countries where they resided.

"His Majesty's Government views with favour the establishment in Palestine of a national home for the Jewish people, and will use its best endeavours to facilitate the achievement of this object . . . "

Contrary to popular misconception, the land of Israel has never been an Arab kingdom from the time of David, being annexed by a succession of empires, the last of which was the Turkish Ottoman Empire. General Allenby captured Jerusalem from the Turks in 1917, without a shot being fired. With the country in British hands, the stage was set for the birth of modern Jewry to create the State of Israel, in their original and Promised Land.

However, the region designated as Palestine by the British, and accepted as being under Britain's mandate by the League of Nations, shrunk very rapidly. In 1921 Churchill sanctioned the creation of Trans-Jordan to appease the Emir and so, in 1923, the current Hashemite kingdom of Jordan was formed. At a stroke this reduced the land available by some 83%, a matter never raised by those arguing over Israel's current borders.

Nonetheless, throughout the twenties and thirties immigration increased, more than 150,000 Jews returning to the land from 1930-1935 alone. Meanwhile, Britain was rapidly losing sight of its original proposals. There is no doubt that much of the policy put forward was the result of expediency. The Government of the United Kingdom believed that placating the Arabs would undermine support for the increasing threat from the German cause. A new white paper outlined a limit of 10,000 Jewish immigrants a year, apart from 25,000 special refugees. This took place at a time when the Foreign Office already knew the pressure European Jewry were beginning to feel as a result of German policies. This was not all, as Gordon Lindsay wrote: "The original tract of 45,000 square miles had been whittled down to 10,000 square miles. Now they could purchase land freely only in an area of 260 square miles."[5]

The suffering of the Jews throughout this period was immense, but in 1945 Germany, Japan and their allies were finally defeated and the Second World War was over. A war-weary country, to the surprise of the Conservative Party and its leader, Winston Churchill, elected a socialist government. But this self-same government, who made so much of their desire for equality and fairness for all, shamefully mistreated many Jews who, in the aftermath of

5   'The Miracle of Israel' - Gordon Lindsay

the war, wished to go to Israel, the one safe haven they saw left open to them.

When one reads accounts of the British Mandate in Palestine in the days after World War Two, one can only feel embarrassment. We subjected a people who had already suffered so much, to the harsh and rigid discipline of what was effectively military rule. It is no surprise that the underground organisations began to conduct a terror campaign against the British. I do not condone their actions, but Britain, at that time still a world power, acted with little compassion towards these sorry and desperate refugees.

There is no doubt that many who had been denied aliyah in the thirties subsequently perished at the hands of the Nazis. That we then refused entry to the pitiful survivors from those places remains a stain on Great Britain to this day. It was appalling that we should forcibly evict men, women and children from the holds of ships that had travelled to Israel and place them in camps on Cyprus. Much of the blame lies at the feet of Ernest Bevin, who refused a request from President Truman to allow another 100,000 refugees to enter. Amazingly it was the Russians, considered hostile to the Jews, who smuggled almost that selfsame number through Black Sea ports and from there to Palestine itself.

President Truman was horrified at Bevin's approach. He said of him; "Underneath his abrasive exterior lies an abrasive interior." Bevin himself told those who lobbied him for a change of policy, "The Jews have waited 2,000 years for a homeland; if they wait a little longer it won't do any harm." In a contrary fashion this may well have helped strengthen Truman's resolve to help the Jews. One of his closest friends persuaded Truman to meet with Chaim Weizmann, but Bevin's intransigence also spurred him into action.

The perverse policy of the British won it few friends either at home or abroad. The Arabs had decided they would be able to sort out the situation to their own satisfaction without the interference of a colonial power. With international opinion swinging against Britain, and with a deteriorating situation on the ground, Britain decided to wash their hands of the problem and allow the UN to resolve the issue.

"The Jews have waited 2,000 years for a homeland; if they wait a little longer it won't do any harm."

Ernest Bevin

On the 29th November, 1947, to the amazement of many seasoned political commentators, a vote supporting the creation of the State of Israel was carried at the UN. It needed a two-thirds majority to gain acceptance. Both Russia and America voted in favour of the resolution. Despite great Arab pressure the only two nations to add their weight to the dissenting voice of the Arabs were Greece and Cuba.

On December 6th, Britain announced the British Mandate would end on May 15th, 1948. At 4.00 p.m. on May 14th, after the British Commissioner had left, the Zionist Council, meeting in Tel-Aviv, declared the inauguration of the State of Israel. President Truman announced that the USA recognised the new state and the country was reborn. It was the signal, if any were needed, for the surrounding Arab nations to attempt to obliterate the fledgling state at its birth.

CHAPTER 21

ISRAEL'S HISTORY
PART TWO:
THE MODERN STATE

"Can a country be born in a day or a nation be brought forth in a moment? Yet no sooner is Zion in labour than she gives birth to her children."

Isaiah 66:8

Within hours of Israel's historic declaration, seven Arab states pitched their armies against this new-born entity, determined to eliminate it before it had a chance to establish itself. The Arabs were well equipped, well armed and well trained, particularly the Jordanian contingent. Intensive fighting took place, but to the surprise of the Arabs, there was no rapid victory. Israel lost most of the city of Jerusalem to the Jordanians, then, after two months of fighting, a ceasefire was agreed on June 11th.

Neither party had any intention of keeping the truce. The Arabs saw it as an opportunity to bolster their troops for a final push against the areas of Jerusalem that remained in Jewish hands, whilst the Jews saw it as a breathing space that would allow them to establish alternative supply routes, and to get their hands on more modern equipment with which to fight their enemies.

Inevitably, given this background, fighting flared up again. A second truce also failed to hold and it wasn't until July 1949 that a more permanent ceasefire could be brokered. In the meantime Jordan had seized the West Bank (annexing it in 1950), declaring it to be part of Jordan. The response of the Arab League was to threaten to expel them, but the war-weary Western powers, already pre-occupied with the communist threat, had no desire to intervene again and so Jordan's area of control increased still further. Egypt meanwhile played much the same game, hanging on to the Gaza strip and its environs as legitimate spoils of war. The above facts should be of vital importance as we listen to current debates castigating Israel for aggression and for refusing to return 'occupied territories.' Most of these self-same territories were illegally occupied by Arab states for almost twenty years, until the 1967 war.

At the same time as the fighting of the late forties erupted, many Arabs were encouraged to leave those areas occupied by Jews, so that the region could be purged before the Arabs returned. This is not to deny the very real intimidation and terror that occurred on both sides, for which some Jews must take responsibility. Again however, it is not commonly recognised that 110,000 Jews were displaced from Arab territories during the fighting, compared with some 100,000 displaced Arabs. The solution to the refugee problem lay firmly in the hand of the Arab nations, but it suited the needs of their rulers to maintain the refugee camps, rather than granting citizenship to the Palestinians. Thus much of the humanitarian crisis was of the making and manufacture of the Arab nations and not of the nation of Israel. Some commentators have observed that in 1949 a week's revenue from the oil-producing Arab states would have solved the Palestinian problem.

Despite those fierce early conflicts, the Israeli state, against all military predictions and to the fury of the Arabs, survived its baptism of fire to emerge into the mid-twentieth century. What was more, with the British gone and the Arabs retiring to lick their wounds, the stage was set for the country to begin to grow and blossom, both industrially and through its burgeoning agricultural machine. Jewish immigration increased. Town after town was rebuilt and it seemed as though the Zionist dream was beginning to take shape.

The Jews were not naïve enough to believe that Arab pride would allow them to continue to exist in this way. Soon Arab boycotts of Israel were being organised. With their great oil wealth, pressure was brought to bear on Israel's trading partners. Eventually the Egyptians tried to close both the Suez Canal and the Tiran Straits to Israel. The plan backfired as this ploy rang alarm bells for the French and British. Concerned over Nasser's increasing influence in the region, his plans for nationalisation of foreign installations and his declared intention to take over the Suez Canal, Britain and France attacked Egypt, with Israel as a partner. For these two European nations it was to be among the last imperial acts of their fading world power, but for Israel it did at least result in free passage through the Straits of Tiran. Despite repeated acts of terrorism, it also succeeded in lessening Egypt's stranglehold for a while.

"The Arab national aim is the
elimination of Israel."
Abdul Nasser: May 1965

Disregarding what he saw as a temporary setback, Nasser set about replanning his strategy. He was determined to be the man who would go down in history as the liberator of Palestine from the Jews. Speaking in May 1965 Nasser said,

"The Arab national aim is the elimination of Israel." The local Egyptian population loved it. Throughout 1966 and the first half of 1967 the posturing and rhetoric went on. It was backed up by troop movements in all the surrounding Arab countries and the shelling of Israeli settlements by the Syrians, from their gun emplacements on the Golan Heights. Finally Egypt ordered the UN observers out of the buffer zone and moved 900 tanks and almost 100,000 troops into Sinai. Once again Egypt closed the Tiran Straits to Israeli shipping. The world waited.

Faced by massive armaments on its borders, on June 5th Israeli forces launched a co-ordinated attack on Egypt's air force, wiping out almost 400 aircraft. Messages were passed to King Hussein from Israel, urging him not to become involved and promising that Israel would not attack Jordan unless first attacked herself. Hussein ignored the offer and Jordanian forces joined in the Arab attacks mounted from the surrounding countries. For Jordan it was a disaster; for Israel the outcome was beyond its wildest dreams.

Within six days Israel crushed the combined Jordanian, Syrian and Egyptian armies, and the contingents from other countries who had joined in on the Arab side. Israel found itself in possession of Sinai, the Golan Heights and all of Jerusalem. What had begun as a war of defence turned into a war of re-unification. For the first time in almost 2,000 years the Jews found themselves the ruling power of all Jerusalem. Israel declared Jerusalem to be the indivisible and eternal capital of Israel. One suspects they were not fully aware of the potency and truth of those words as they uttered them.

Years before, Chaim Weizmann, speaking to the UN had said this: "God made a promise to give all of Palestine to the Jews; it is up to God to keep His promise in His own time." Another part of the promise was being fulfilled. Jesus had said to His disciples: *"Jerusalem will be trampled on by the Gentiles until the times of the Gentiles are fulfilled."*[1] The world was not yet aware of it, but that time had now come.

Many nations, despite God's Word, are still attempting to decide the fate of Israel and Jerusalem, taking what they see as the moral high ground as they lecture Israel on what it should do. They and their leaders are doomed to failure. Speaking through the prophet Zechariah, God said this: *"I am going to make Jerusalem a cup that sends all the surrounding peoples reeling. Judah will be besieged as well as Jerusalem. On that day, when all the nations are gathered against her, I will make Jerusalem an immovable rock for all the nations. All who try to move it will injure themselves."*[2] In the years since the Six day War resolution after resolution has been passed condemning Israel. God will not be indifferent to this politicking, but He will answer the nations in His own time.

It would be good to be able to say that the Six Day War brought an end to hostilities but, as the Bible had made clear, that was not to be the case. As we know from history, guerrilla attacks continued and a war of attrition existed. By 1973, re-armed and re-equipped with far more sophisticated equipment, including a Soviet-supplied umbrella of air defence systems that they thought would neutralise the Israeli air force, the Arab states were ready to go to war again. The Yom Kippur War was to be no repeat of the Six Day War. It's easy, with the benefit of hindsight, to sit down and write about Israeli arrogance and complacency, but one senses God needed to show His people He was still the one who was their protector.

On the holiest day in the Jewish calendar, the Day of Atonement, the one time when even the most secular of Jews are not working, the Arab armies attacked. Much vaunted defence systems along the Suez Canal were breached or by-passed by the Egyptian army, the few defenders being unable to resist the tide that swept towards them. Syria and

1   Luke 21:24
2   Zechariah 12:1-3

Egypt, who attacked simultaneously, had over 1,000,000 troops between them. The Syrian force was backed up by Iraqis, Jordanians, Moroccans and other contingents. The Israelis were resigned to losses, hoping at least to deal with the Syrian attacks first.

> "God made a promise to give all of Palestine to the Jews; it is up to God to keep His promise in His own time."
>
> Chaim Weizmann

Amazingly, providentially, the Egyptians halted their advance, allowing the Israelis to regroup. Meanwhile, after fierce fighting, the armies allied to Syria were repulsed and Damascus came under attack. Israel now began to turn its attention to the Egyptian forces. From a position of strength the Egyptian Third Army suddenly found itself outmanoeuvred, encircled and isolated, open to the mercy of Israeli forces. Cairo was virtually defenceless. However, once Israel had gained the upper hand immense pressure was brought to bear upon her to withdraw and let the Egyptian army escape. Reluctantly she complied. Once more, against all the odds, Israel had survived a major conflict with her neighbours.

As the seventies continued, Jordan, in bloody fighting, expelled the Palestinians from the West Bank. A mass exodus of Palestinian fighters fled to Lebanon in search of a new home and were a major cause of the civil war that broke out in that region. We should remind ourselves again that of the territory set aside for a national homeland for the Jewish people, over 35,000 square miles (out of the 46,000 square miles allocated) had been given to the Hashemite kingdom of Jordan. Ignoring Biblical considerations for a moment, pure human reasoning suggests that any further land claims for the dispossessed Arab population, should have come from this area.

The years that followed brought continued attacks against Israel, from Jordan, Egypt and most notably Lebanon. The massing of PLO fighters in Lebanon, armed and supplied by a coalition of the Iraqis and Syrians, led to one of the most controversial episodes in modern Jewish warfare, the invasion of Lebanon.

Lebanon itself had not been immune from infighting. In the years preceding Israel's invasion, 120,000 people had been killed in what was virtually a war between warlords. After repeated attacks on Israeli settlements and villages, including over 2,000 rockets aimed at Israeli settlements in a single month, Israeli patience snapped in 1982. When the Israelis went in they uncovered vast quantities of arms and discovered Soviet-backed bases dedicated to world terrorism.

Hardly any of this found its way into the press. Instead there were pictures of a blitzed Beirut. Much of the damage had been done in the years prior to the invasion, but was conveniently not mentioned by reporters after a 'good' story. The reporting of the war began to show an increasingly hostile attitude towards Israel, painting her as the aggressor and bully. Meanwhile the regimes in Syria and Iraq (and subsequently Iran) were virtually ignored, though their sponsorship of terrorism, their ambition to control the whole region and their desire to foment unrest were well known.

At the same time the PLO and their allies began to discover the power of the media. Through careful 'spinning' they could present themselves as moderate and oppressed, while the Jews could be portrayed as arrogant warmongers. Arabs could be seen as reasonable and Jews as merely stubborn.

Basic human rights might not exist in their countries, but as long as the story was believed, who was going to worry over such detail?

Since the early eighties Israel has continued to live on the knife-edge of war. Iraq threatened its annihilation in the first Gulf War and Syria continues to use its puppet terrorist groups to harass and embarrass Israel. Even Jordan, regarded by the West as so moderate and respectable, looks for its own ends. Jordan sided with Saddam Hussein in the first Gulf War. The PLO, Hizbollah and an increasingly confident Hamas continue to challenge Israel's right to exist.

The Oslo Peace Accord carried Israel a step further down the line to final confrontation with the Palestinians. It is as though the world shuts its eyes to reality when dealing with Israel.

Ezekiel talks of *malicious neighbours.* I believe Israel has malicious neighbours. Yet there are those, our own governments included, who invite these malicious neighbours to talks and who insist Israel give up yet more land, land given by divine right. Writing in 1980, Teddy Kollek, then mayor of Jerusalem, observed: "One of the greatest dangers . . . to the attainment of peace in the Middle East is the PLO . . . By logic the Arabs of Jerusalem, as well as the Arabs on the West Bank in the Gaza Strip, should be our natural partners in the search for peace. But what chance do they have as long as the international community, and especially the Europeans, persist in their infatuation with the PLO . . . I have no doubt that unless the governments of Western Europe and elsewhere desist from their policy of boosting the PLO, the terrorist organisation will continue successfully to intimidate and assassinate the moderate Palestinian elements, thus making peace an even more illusory goal."

Even now, after the debacle of the withdrawal from Lebanon and the so-called intifada, there are those who insist Israel should make peace and take the risks involved. The inevitable outcome will be yet further conflict. The Bible urges the Jewish people to welcome foreigners and strangers who live among them, but not if they ultimately seek Israel's destruction.

Sadly, Teddy Kollek's words concerning the PLO and succeeding militant groups have proved only too true. The so-called 'land for peace' initiatives will at best bring an illusory calm while fresh forces gather against Israel. Further wars are inevitable. They may be even more bloody and brutal than previous ones. Jesus said: *"You will hear of wars and rumours of wars, but see to it that you are not alarmed."*[3] As we face the countdown to the final stage of world history before Christ's return, what will our response to all these events be? It needs to be—Watch and Pray.

3   Matthew 24:6

Chapter 22

ISRAEL AND ITS EMERGING MESSIANIC CONGREGATIONS

"Do not be afraid, O worm Jacob, O little Israel, for I Myself will help you," declares the LORD, your Redeemer, the Holy One of Israel.

Isaiah 41:14

What then, of the Christian Church in Israel? There have been Christian missionary societies operating in Israel for at least the last 150 years, prominent amongst them the Lutherans and Baptists. The most notable, a mix of the philanthropic and the spiritual, has been the Churches Ministry Among the Jews, sponsored through Anglican circles. To a large extent these missionary groups have been more successful in their philanthropic work than in their mission aims, though there have been occasional bright spots in what was a generally barren landscape for the church. By the fifties and sixties they had, to a large extent, either ceased to exist, fallen back into good works or were providing education and a haven for European and American families who found themselves in the region.

The Six Day War was something of a watershed. After its conclusion reports of the occasional conversion trickled through. Unfortunately Jewish believers in Jesus were all too often paraded like sporting trophies—a situation not helpful to either the individuals involved or those who sought to disciple them.

By the early eighties there were a number of small and struggling congregations in Israel, though you could probably have counted their total on both hands. They still tended to be comprised of ex-patriates. Among the Jewish population, believers in Jesus, as Messiah, were still hard to find.

Jewish believers in Jesus were all too often paraded like sporting trophies—a situation not helpful to either the individuals involved or those who sought to disciple them.

Now however, in the early years of the twenty-first century, you can count the number of fellowships in tens, some congregations in hundreds, and believers in the land in their thousands. To a large extent this growth has been fuelled by the mass immigration of Jews from the former Soviet Union and from countries such as Ethiopia, who have either arrived as believers, or who are far more open to the gospel. Among sabras (native-born Jews) the response is still extremely limited, but the trickle has become a stream, and one day it will become a river. To the credit of some of the missionary societies already mentioned, this has also come about through a transfer of leadership (and land and property) to indigenous congregations.

These fellowships still live in something of a goldfish bowl, gawped at or held up as fascinating sideshows by visiting

Christians from around the world. They have their own problems, as do all young churches, but they are beginning to mature and God is raising up leaders among them.

Like the rest of the population, they are not immune to the wearing strain of living in a country that can seem under siege. They have to serve in the armed forces in the same way as do all other Israeli citizens. They have to do all this in the light of an uncertain future for the land and of a critical international community. They are not immune to the material world and the moral flavour of a country that is neither more, nor less, decadent than many other societies. Like large sections of the Church, they are not always discerning about doctrine, or about the motives of those who bring 'ministry', but God still has His hand upon them.

They face enormous pressures. They are an affront to the ultra-religious and orthodox, and a threat to vestiges of the traditional Eastern and Western churches in the country. They come from vastly differing cultural backgrounds and so can struggle to be accepted or to fit into Israeli society. In the spiritual realm they must be anathema to all that Satan is attempting to do. They are a mark, if you like, of God's continuing faithfulness to His people. For these, and a plethora of other reasons, they need our prayerful support.

Chapter 23

A PRAYERFUL WATCH
OVER ISRAEL

I have posted watchmen on your walls, O Jerusalem; they will
never be silent day or night. You who call on the LORD, give
yourselves no rest, and give Him no rest till He establishes
Jerusalem and makes her the praise of the earth.

Isaiah 62:6-7

Our introduction to this study of the land and people of Israel
began by telling us: *At that time men began to call upon the*
name of the LORD.[1] Through both the Old and New
Testaments, we find men of faith praying before God. Every
biblical figure who is presented as a good example to us,
understood what it meant to know God through prayer. From
Abraham, Isaac and Jacob, through to David, Josiah, Isaiah to
Malachi, we read how these men of God presented their
petitions to the Lord.

The things for which they came to God were not abstract, but
were concerned with the circumstances of their lives and of
the lives of those around them. Often they found themselves
led to pray for situations in which they found themselves;
situations where only the power of the Lord could rescue
them or change their perspective.

Daniel, as we have seen previously, understood, from his
reading of Jeremiah's prophecies, that the time for Jewish
captivity in Babylon was coming to an end. He came to God

1 Genesis 4:26

on that basis and pleaded for the people. He identified himself with their sin and their need for forgiveness. He stood as an intercessor for them.

In the New Testament we are told that Jesus, our Great High Priest, ever lives to make intercession for us. Through Jesus we too can come to God and intercede. The basis of that intercession is our faith in Him and in the power of His blood and resurrection. Paul wrote: *Therefore brothers, since we have confidence to enter the Most Holy Place by the blood of Jesus, by a new and living way opened for us through the curtain, that is, His body, and since we have a Great Priest over the house of God, let us draw near to God with a sincere heart in full assurance of faith, having our hearts sprinkled to cleanse us from a guilty conscience and having our bodies washed with pure water.*[2]

Lining ourselves up with God's promises will open our eyes and encourage our faith and prayer.

We are also told that if we approach God and ask anything according to His plan He will grant it. We have seen from our study that God has a plan and a purpose for the salvation of the Jews.

- Presuming that we believe in evangelism, it should not then be a problem for us to approach God on the basis of seeing that salvation.

- Furthermore, we know that God has a plan to restore His people to the land of Israel, so we may pray for that also.

- Thirdly, assuming we read the newspapers or listen to the news, we will be able to understand the spiritual

2 Hebrews 10:19-22

forces behind events affecting World Jewry and be able to pray for the protection and deliverance of the Jewish people.

- Fourthly, if we understand that all of this takes place because we serve a covenant-keeping God, we will come to Him on the basis of those covenants and promises.

Lining ourselves up with God's promises will open our eyes and encourage our faith and prayer. That should not be confused with praying for, or supporting, everything that is Jewish. In the same way I trust we do not support everything that purports to be Christian in origin. God does not need us to distort and confuse issues but to pray on the basis of His revealed will, found through the Bible.

We are called to have discernment and understanding. May we use that discernment and understanding as we pray for the veil to be taken from the eyes of God's people, the Jews. And let us, as part of the Christian community, be ready to give practically and serve in helping to bring God's ancient people, the Jews, back to the land that is theirs as *"an everlasting possession."*[3] As we do that, I believe we will enter into a fuller understanding of the purposes God has for the Church and the Jewish nation—the preparation for the return of the One who is (and will be visibly) the King of Kings—The Lord Jesus Christ.

3   Genesis 17:8

TRIBAL ALLOTMENTS

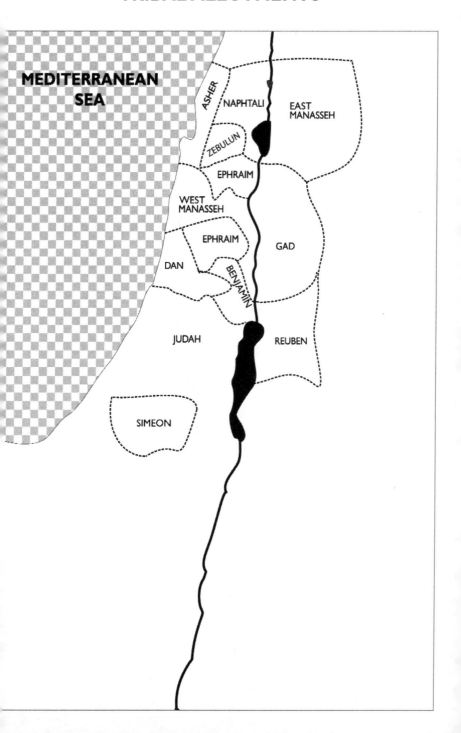

THE KINGDOM UNDER DAVID AND SOLOMON

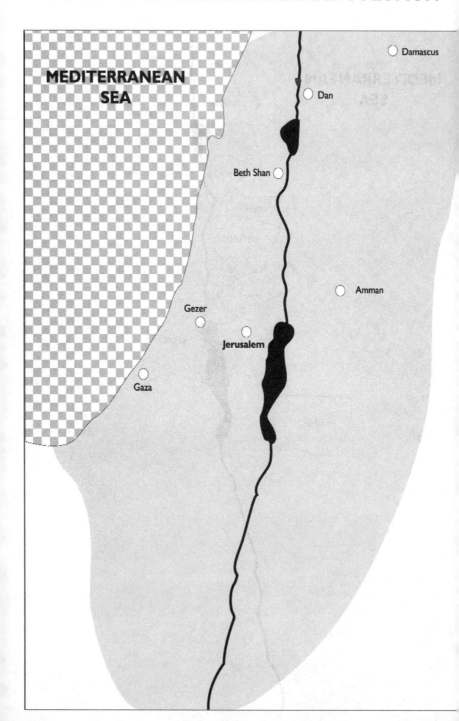

THE DIVIDED KINGDOM

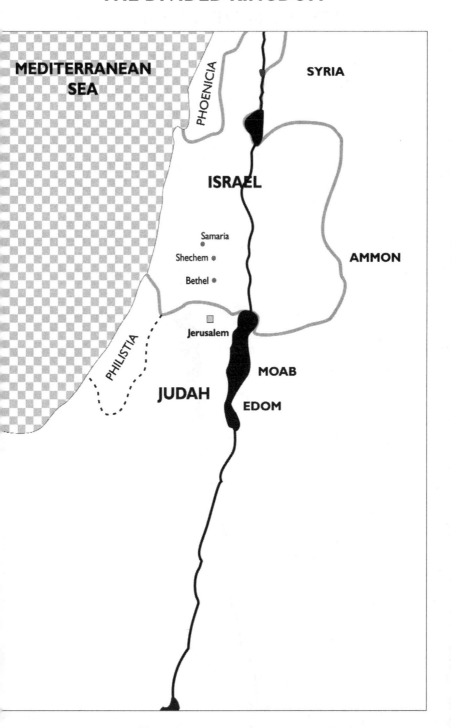

ISRAEL (PALESTINE) UNDER THE OTTOMAN EMPIRE 1517 - 1917

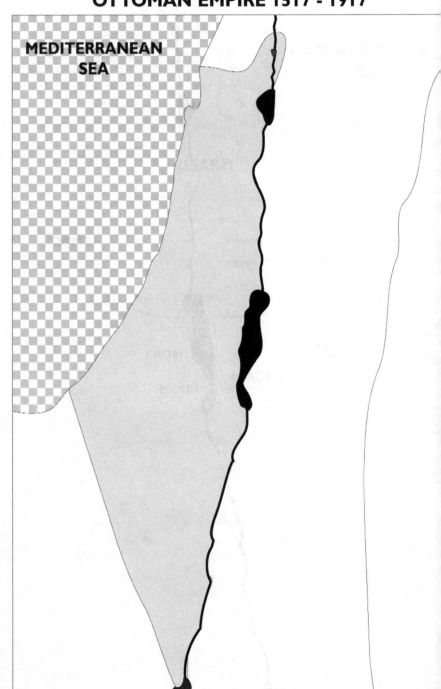

MEDITERRANEAN
SEA

PALESTINE AS DEFINED UNDER THE BALFOUR DECLARATION

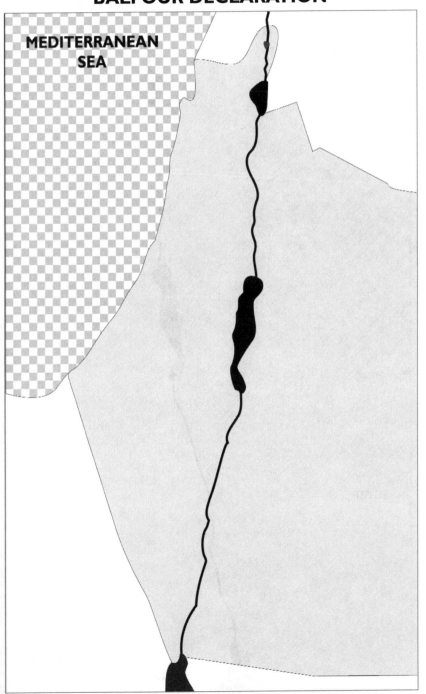

MEDITERRANEAN
SEA

ISRAEL (PALESTINE) AND JORDAN AFTER ITS DIVISION BY THE BRITISH (1923 - 1948)

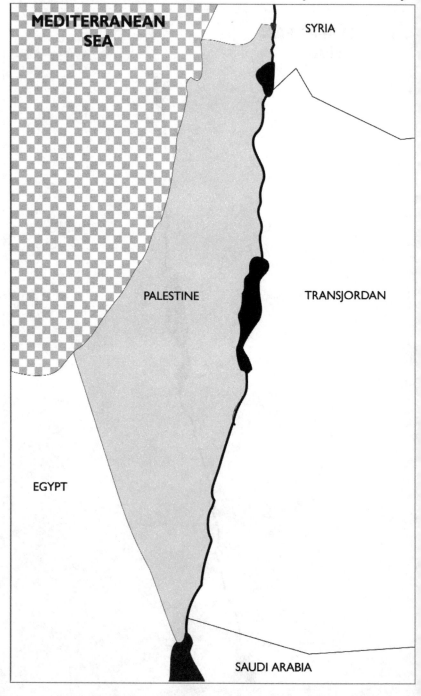

ISRAEL UNDER THE PARTITION PLAN
OF 29TH NOVEMBER 1947

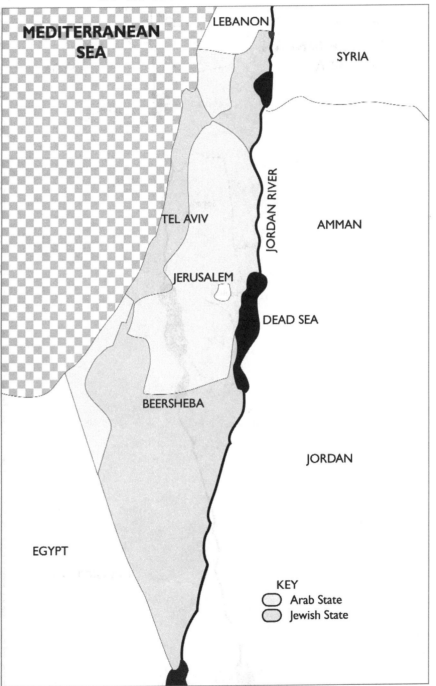

ISRAEL AFTER THE 1948-1949 WAR

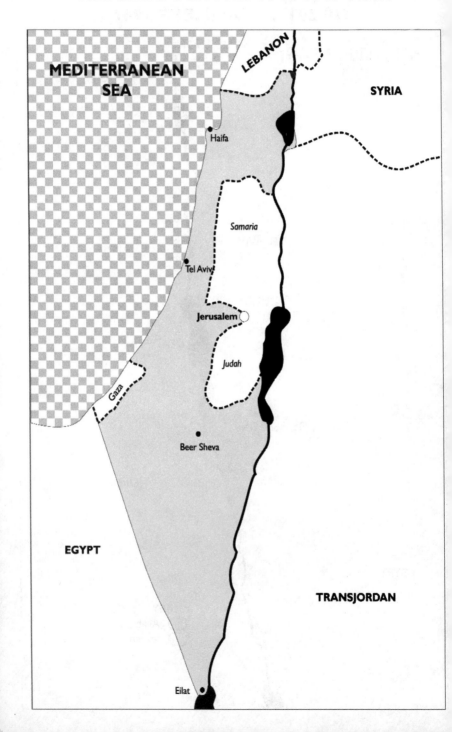

ISRAEL AFTER THE 1967 WAR

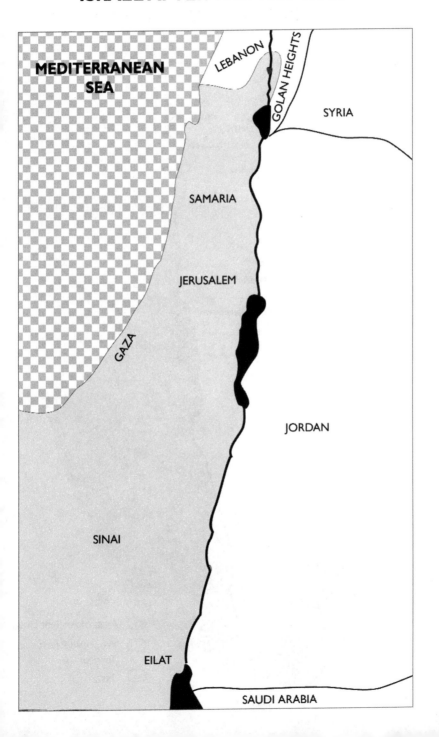

MODERN ISRAEL AND PROPOSED PALESTINIAN TERRITORIES

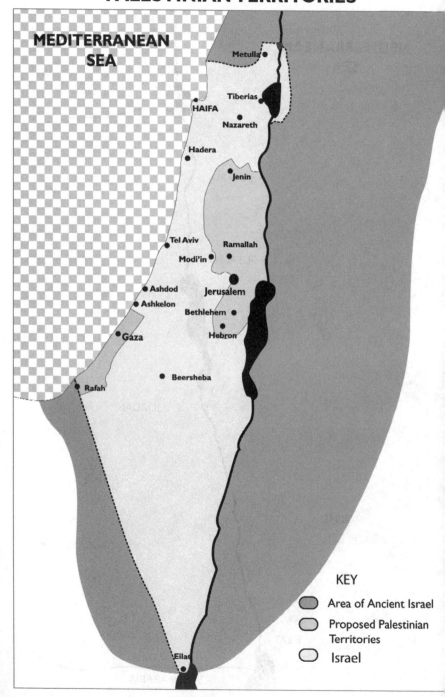

MEDITERRANEAN
SEA

Metulla

Tiberias

HAIFA

Nazareth

Hadera

Jenin

Tel Aviv

Ramallah

Modi'in

Ashdod

Jerusalem

Ashkelon

Bethlehem

Gaza

Hebron

Rafah

Beersheba

Eilat

KEY

Area of Ancient Israel

Proposed Palestinian
Territories

Israel